ACQUIRING AND DEVELOPING CHURCH REAL ESTATE

CHURCH BUSINESS MANAGEMENT SERIES

ACQUIRING AND DEVELOPING CHURCH REAL ESTATE

Joseph Stiles

PRENTICE-HALL, INC.

Englewood Cliffs, New Jersey

PRENTICE-HALL INTERNATIONAL, INC., *London*
PRENTICE-HALL OF AUSTRALIA, PTY., LTD., *Sydney*
PRENTICE-HALL OF CANADA, LTD., *Toronto*
PRENTICE-HALL OF INDIA (PRIVATE) LTD., *New Delhi*
PRENTICE-HALL OF JAPAN, INC., *Tokyo*

EDITOR'S INTRODUCTION

THE PURPOSE of the series of books in which this volume is included is to provide new insight and specific guidance for managing effectively the affairs of churches and related non-profit organizations. These books represent the most comprehensive publishing project ever completed in the field of church management.

Each volume in this series is based on four major premises: First, if churches are to accomplish their distinctive purposes, their approaches to management must be at least as effective as those of other organizations. Second, some of the principles of management that are applied satisfactorily in business, government, hospitals, and elsewhere may be used appropriately and effectively in churches. Third, since churches are service-rendering rather than profit-making, and because of the uniqueness of their voluntary nature and trustee relationship, some of their management policies and practices must be different from those of commercial enterprises. Fourth, the differences between management approaches that are designed for secular organizations and management approaches that are relevant to the purposes of churches must be clearly identified and thoroughly understood.

5

These books are intended to (1) help clergy and laity develop additional competence for effective stewardship of church management responsibilities, (2) provide stimulation and practical suggestions for professional career service as directors or ministers of management, and (3) make available an educational basis for strengthening the role of pastors as chief administrators of individual churches.

In designing and preparing the material for this series of books the editor and the authors were confronted with basic questions to which answers had not been published. What *is* church management? What is it *for?* What is it *not?* What is it *not* for? What are its boundaries and its components? The following formulation is a result of the editor's pioneer effort to identify and delineate this field:

> *Church Management* is the science and art of administering church program development, financial resources, physical facilities, office services, staff personnel, and program promotion—according to effective standards of religious stewardship. Included in this concept are such managerial processes as forecasting, planning, organizing, delegating, controlling, and reporting. Church management is a facilitating function and should be regarded not as an end in itself but as an important means to an end.

Many alert and imaginative congregations in recent years have added to the employed staff a qualified career-service director or minister of management. Usually he is a person of considerable maturity, religious commitment, management experience, and relevant training. He serves as a professional consultant and resource leader in helping church officers and staff, both volunteers and employees, perform their administrative duties in relation to the ministry of:

1. *Program Development*—planning, organizing, and scheduling all appropriate means available to the church for accomplishing its objectives and goals.
2. *Financial Management*—obtaining, allocating, safeguarding, disbursing, and accounting for all monetary resources.
3. *Property Management*—using, maintaining, and acquiring buildings, grounds, furniture, and equipment.
4. *Office Management*—providing systematic programs of scheduling, communicating, recording, and reporting designed to facilitate performance of other administrative functions.
5. *Personnel Management*—determining and describing staff positions; enlisting, assigning, and training staff personnel, both volunteers and employees; developing and maintaining staff morale.
6. *Program Promotion*—communicating the church's concept of its objectives, goals, accomplishments, potentialities, and needs.

Church management as viewed in this light, and when applied creatively through collaborative and democratic processes, may be regarded as a significant phase of a meaningful spiritual ministry. How effectively the author of each book in this series has amplified the foregoing philosophy may be determined by the readers themselves.

For invaluable advice and practical assistance throughout the planning and execution stages of this endeavor the editor is grateful to Dr. Nathan A. Baily, dean of the School of Business Administration, The American University. Dean Baily's keen interest and capable leadership stimulated the establishment of the Center for Church Business Management while facilitating the development of this series of books.

Clyde W. Humphrey
General Editor

Washington, D.C.

ACKNOWLEDGMENTS

I AM deeply indebted to many people for assistance in preparing this volume. As one of the great poets has said, "I am a part of all that I have met"; hence, all the information and most of the insights here expressed were obtained from others. Much came from books, articles, and pamphlets. Where quotations are lifted, or where sole sources can be identified, credit is given. However, most of the insights have been validated by the author through his years of experience as pastor-leader in guiding church improvement and expansion programs for both small and large congregations.

In a particular way I would like to thank Dr. W. A. Harrell, Secretary of the Church Architecture Department, Southern Baptist Sunday School Board, Nashville, Tennessee, who for a quarter of a century has been a good friend and teacher. I am grateful to him for the encouragement he has given me as well as for permission to use some of the materials produced by his department. Dean Allen W. Graves of the School of Religious Education, Southern Baptist Theological Seminary, also has given helpful advice. Mr. Frank C. Dill, A. I. A., Houston, Texas, an architect with broad church experience, has read portions of the material and made valuable suggestions.

Appreciation is also expressed to Mrs. James Hughes for her good work in typing and retyping the manuscript.

I shall be happy if the result of this effort helps even one church fulfill more completely its responsibility in Christ's Kingdom.

Joseph Stiles

Louisville, Kentucky

CONTENTS

CONTENTS

Chapter 1

THE WHAT AND WHY OF THIS BOOK

THIS BOOK is one in a series of volumes on church management. The guiding thought of the author is that there are two basic elements in the administrative process: (1) adopting objectives, and (2) developing means of achieving the objectives. Acquiring and developing church real estate are definitely means. Investment in land and buildings can be justified only when this is done for the purpose of achieving the primary objectives of the church.

Jesus stated clearly two basic objectives of a church when he said "go therefore and make disciples of all the nations . . . and teach them to observe every command which I have given you" (Matt. 28:19-20 [Weymouth]). "Making disciples" is evangelizing or witnessing. "Teaching them to observe" is nurture or education. The author undertakes to deal with the acquiring and developing of church real estate in such a way as to further these two objectives. Hence, the winning of disciples and developing them into effective Christians are the author's basic reasons for writing this book.

This volume is concerned with development of facilities that relate directly to the functioning of a local congrega-

13

tion as it seeks to fulfill its purpose. No attempt is made to deal with church real estate and its development in relation to colleges, hospitals, orphanages, and other church-related agencies. Limited treatment is given to encampments or assemblies, because these also are means by which a church seeks to achieve its aims of evangelism and education. Although many of the principles and procedures described here may well apply to other institutions involved in enlargement, that has not been our purpose.

Most churches need extensive remodeling and enlargement of their physical facilities. Thousands of churches each year undertake expansion programs to care for the increasing numbers of people for whom they are responsible. In every case, the pastor and a committee of laymen assume the unusual task of guiding a congregation through the difficult and trying experience of acquiring and improving real estate for the service of their church. Only a few of them have had adequate experience and specific training for the task. The author's purpose is to try to give a clear explanation of planning and building procedures that will serve as a guide to church building committees as they seek to accomplish their mission.

WHY

There are many good reasons that a book of this kind is needed. For one thing, church building is big business. The Department of Commerce predicts that the amount of money spent annually on church buildings in the United States soon will go beyond the one billion-dollar mark. Few people realize the magnitude of the Christian effort. In a recent year 256,218 Protestant Sunday Schools were reported. More than 35,000,000 persons were enrolled, which was 500,000 more than were enrolled that year in the public schools of the nation. Yet, this is only a small percentage of the people who could be helped by regular worship and Bible study. The magnitude of this effort indicates its great importance.

A second reason for writing this book is that churches, more than other organizations, are prone to plunge into a program of real-estate acquisition and development without adequate study and preparation. This point may be illustrated by the fact that a certain church, having discussed its need of more space for its education program, appointed a small committee to give the matter further consideration. One member of the committee, who had an engineering background, went immediately to his drafting board and prepared a floor plan for a rectangular building about 30 by 60 feet with two partitions making three rooms of equal size. The next day he brought the sketch to the pastor and said, "Pastor, here is a drawing of a building that I feel we can make good use of." This faithful member was eager to help through use of his talents, but he had overlooked the importance of determining the needs of the program before planning a building for it.

Construction of church buildings is important for another reason. Most churches undertake a major expansion program not more than once in a generation. This means that few people have more than one opportunity to participate directly in the development of a building for the glory of God and for the work of His Kingdom. This fact alone should inspire both clergy and laity to do creditable work in planning and constructing church buildings. No one should be content to do less than his best with such an opportunity.

In addition, church buildings have significant cultural values for society. They should be the most inspiring and most advantageously located buildings in the community. Buildings erected for God should give a continuing though silent witness to the faith of a congregation, so that all who view them may be challenged to the highest and best. Such buildings can and should be a blessing both to those who enter and to those who pass by. To plan something mediocre is unworthy of the opportunity.

The changing social situation demands more and better church buildings. The growth and movement of population is a constant challenge. Many, if not most, church buildings are obsolete and ill adapted to present needs. Some churches are being choked to death by poor location and inadequate physical facilities. A generation or two ago, a one-room building that provided a place for a preaching service was considered adequate. Now people need an expanded ministry from their church because of the increasing stresses of modern life. Thousands of completely new congregations will be needed to meet the challenge of the coming multitudes. By 1980 the population of the United States is expected to be 250 million. This is almost exactly the estimated number of people in the whole world when Jesus said, "Go and make disciples."

The importance of church physical facilities is seen more clearly when we realize the extent to which they determine the church program. To perform broader ministries, the congregation and staff must have a place to work and meet and serve. The number of people reached and the ministries provided are limited to a great extent by the adequacy of building and equipment. Rally days and special seasons may overcrowd the facilities occasionally, but unless adequate facilities provide the newcomers with reasonable comfort and convenience, they will not continue to come.

Another reason for the great importance of adequate church buildings is that church building is God's business. Since the Church is a spiritual institution, its mission in the world is most important. Scientific laboratories and commercial plants have produced powerful machines and weapons. Whether these creations are curses or blessings depends upon the spirit of the person who directs their use. The Church is dealing with the human spirit, which is the most powerful, and in some ways the most dangerous, as well as the most difficult to guide of all the forces in the world. The Church is endeavoring to bring human personality, with all its potentialities for good or evil, under the transforming and guiding influence of God through Jesus Christ. The responsibility for providing physical facilities for such a purpose is a challenge to the best talents and the highest intelligence.

Chapter 2

DETERMINING THE NEEDS

AN EFFECTIVE CHURCH is one that meets the spiritual needs of its constituents. Whether it be large or small, its vitality comes from the grass roots of community demands. Life has a way of rejecting and discarding the irrelevant. If a church's existence depends upon its meeting the needs of people, these needs must be known, so that plans can be made to meet them. Before launching any significant expansion program, a church must get the answers to such very important questions as:

1. What is the church trying to do?
2. With what needs of the community should the church be concerned?
3. How well is the church meeting the needs of the community?
4. What is the church's basic strategy for accomplishing its purposes?
5. What buildings and grounds are needed for accomplishing the purposes of the church?

THE MISSION OF THE CHURCH

The first question, "What is the church trying to do?" is a theological question that should undergird and give direction to all planning and program development. The reasons for building are much more important than the structure itself. Many serious building problems have come because more time was spent thinking about buildings than about the reasons for them. The building is never an end in itself, but only an important means through which the church hopes to serve its purposes.

That every church rethink its purpose is not only fitting but imperative. Christianity is facing a tragic situation. After 1,900 years of effort by the Church, the world is becoming increasingly non-Christian. The rapid increase in non-Christian population and the steady encroachment of secularism into all moral and spiritual values suggest the need to seek the answer to the question, "Why are we here and what are we supposed to be doing?" Especially is this true when a church considers a major program of enlargement or improvement.

The mission of the Church has been expressed in many ways. When Jesus said, "I will build my church," he revealed his intention that the Church would carry out his purpose in the world. The statement "God was in Christ reconciling the world to himself" tells the story. The people of God must have the purpose of God which is, through Christ, to bring a message and a ministry of reconciliation. Man, because of his own willful disobedience, is estranged from God and needs to be reconciled to a loving and saving Lord. Christ is the Reconciler. The Church must witness to this truth. To undertake seriously this task involves a program of worship, of teaching, and of fellowship that can hardly be carried on without a suitable and adequate place for service and meetings.

The greatest danger is that the Church might feel satisfied with what is being done. The greatest need is that the Church would take Jesus seriously and get enthusiastically involved in following his instructions to make disciples and teach them to observe all things that

he commanded. The first-century disciples did exactly
that. So powerful and effective was their witness that it
was said of them that "they have turned the world upside
down." The churches of every community today need to
recapture the sense of mission of the early Church that
earned such a compliment from their enemies. J. B. Phillips, after working fifteen years in translating the New
Testament from the original language, gives the following
description of the activity of that early Church:

> The early vigorous Church was essentially a working,
> serving, and forward-looking Church . . . It expanded
> and spread into all sorts of unlikely places armed only
> with the Good News of the love and power of the Spirit
> . . . The time had not yet come for any church to become
> inward-looking, prosperous, or self-satisfied. . . .
>
> Sometimes nowadays one gets the impression that the
> Christians exist in a closed circle of fellowship, with all
> their members facing inward, while behind their backs
> there are the millions who long, albeit unconsciously, for
> the Gospel, and for the point and purpose in life that only
> the Gospel can bring. If the churches are to recover the
> vast power and influence of the Church of the New Testa-
> ment times, there must be a fundamental change of
> attitude in many churches which means, of course, a funda-
> mental change in the attitude of the churches' members.
> We must recover our sense of vocation, our sense that we
> are not, as I said above, an organization of people who
> have a common interest in religion, but the local repre-
> sentatives of the God whom we serve and of the Heaven
> to which we belong." [1]

Every congregation should make a self-study and come
to a decision as to what it ought to be and do. If a church

[1] J. B. Phillips, *New Testament Christianity* (New York: The Mac-
millan Company, 1956), pp. 98-99.

decides that it is merely an "organization of people with a common interest in religion," it will not need the same kind of facilities that will be needed if a church sees itself as the local representatives of Almighty God, sharing his message of redemption and reconciliation with every needy soul in the community. Whatever view of the Church is held by any particular congregation will greatly affect the nature and size of facilities needed.

If we are to construct really good church buildings, our deepest dedication must not be to architecture and beauty, but to Jesus Christ the Lord, and to the furthering of the work of His Kingdom.

STUDY THE COMMUNITY

There are many wrong ways to get started in a program of expansion. A church may empower a small committee to proceed with a building according to its own view. Equally wrong is the procedure of canvassing the membership to see what the majority of the congregation wants. Not much better would be the plan to hire an architect and leave it all to him. To send the officers to find out how much money can be raised or borrowed is altogether wrong.

The better way is to begin with a study committee. This committee may be designated the survey committee, or the long-range planning committee, or any other suitable name. Of special importance is its function or purpose, which should be to study carefully the community needs and the church ministry before launching any kind of building program. The size of such a committee may vary. In a small church, ten or twelve may suffice, but in a larger church, as many as thirty or more may well be used. It certainly should be representative of the whole congregation and should be comprised of the most dedicated and most imaginative members of the church. This committee is responsible for obtaining definite answers to some very difficult questions, such as:

1. What is the character and composition of the community we are to serve?
2. What social forces affecting its character must be reckoned with?
3. What changes can be expected to affect our ministry, and how soon?
4. How well is the church living up to its present responsibilities?
5. Is the program adequate to meet the need of all groups in the community?
6. Is the program developing members and leaders who will maintain the work in the future?
7. Is the property adequate to meet the needs today and tomorrow?
8. How can present facilities be used more effectively?

A church needs facts, not guesses, about its opportunities and resources before entering an expensive program of enlargement.

Many churches would consider such a study to be an impossible task, but once a start is made, ample resources become available. In every community, relevant materials are available and agencies are able and willing to help. In libraries, materials of all kinds are accumulated. The census reports provide not only population statistics but also average family income and racial composition of each political unit. Public schools can furnish detailed information of school-age constituents. Colleges and universities often make intensive studies of particular communities and situations. Progressive chambers of commerce make it a point to know the conditions in order to project their plans. Planning commissions in growing cities may know years in advance where the highways, the schools, and other important projects will be. Police departments make careful record of the incidence of crime and delinquency in each area. Public utilities provide much useful information. The telephone company plans for expansion far in advance of the present needs. Church councils and denominational organizations gather significant data in order to plan wisely for new churches.

Professional guidance in such a survey may be helpful, but it is not essential. In almost every church, qualified leaders can be found who would be willing to make a self-study. The challenge of a unique and fresh undertaking may uncover leadership talent not previously recognized.

In 1959, Christ Congregational Church of Silver Spring, Maryland, conducted a self-study of many aspects of its church life and made reports and recommendations on each. This study group was divided into the following committees: church membership, church neighborhood, church program, church staff and lay leadership, church finance, and church building and equipment. Subcommittees or divisions of responsibility could be arranged to meet the needs of any particular situation.

The committee to study the church neighborhood may find that social changes are an unfailing certainty. Changes in a community may come rapidly, or they may occur almost imperceptibly. No one knows his community unless he has recently made a careful study of it.

Boundaries should be determined. The community may have some natural boundaries such as rivers, mountains, highways, railroads, and drainage canals. Such barriers often restrict a church's outreach. Boundaries may also be logically based upon agreements with other churches or on decisions of the church itself to limit its outreach to a reasonable distance. There may be social boundaries.

Within a community there may be neighborhoods with social distinctiveness that is hard to overcome. The committee should check all the adjoining areas to determine whether the field should be extended to include them.

Population is most important and will be the main concern. A chart showing population trends for several decades should be made. The United States census report gives statistics by voting precincts. By comparing with previous reports, the rate of growth or decline and changes in the racial makeup of a community will be apparent. Any considerable change in ratios may be significant. To learn the characteristics of the residents as to sex, age, religion, and types of occupations will add greatly to the clarity of the picture.

If accurate population figures are not readily available, present population may be estimated by counting the number of homes and multiplying by the average number in each family. Another easy way is to check with the electric company to learn how many residential meters are in a given area. Utility companies usually permit only one family per meter. Recent United States census reports give average incomes, home evaluations, age divisions, and other helpful brackets of information.

But it is not enough to know about the people who are there today. What the population will become is extremely important. The rapid growth of cities and metropolitan areas calls for long-range strategy. Undeveloped lots and acres may need to be considered. One committee seeking this information counted the number of vacant lots in the partially developed area. It was not difficult to project these facts into the probable potential population of a growing section of a great metropolis.

The national population figures regarding trends in various age groups are quite startling. It is estimated that

by 1970 there will be in this country 3½ million more boys
and girls between the ages of 13 and 16. There will be 9
million more young people between the ages of 17 and 24.
By 1970, there will be 20 million adults 65 years old and
above, and most of these will be in good health and
economically independent. Births have been averaging
more than 4 million per year. When the war babies born
in the 1940's marry and have their families (as has already
begun), there will be rapid increases in children's groups
for years to come.

The challenge to provide a spiritual ministry for these
multitudes must be met. The situation demands more
churches with larger and better facilities planned to reach
and meet the needs of the various groupings as they appear in each church field. It is readily seen that a church
must know its field and its potential to plan wisely for expansion.

Religious patterns should be known. To forecast church
building needs, the religious composition of a community
must be determined. The study committee should find out
how many constituents of various religious denominations
live in the community. Trends may be determined by
making a comparison with the figures of former years.
Changes often come unnoticed. The needs may not be
the same as they were. For example: A church experienced a rapid growth during the early years of its life. Although the growth of the community continued, the
church growth stopped. The pastor received criticism for
slackness in the growth of the church, and some members
were ready for a new leader. A careful house-to-house
survey revealed that the religious character of the community had changed. A large church and parochial school
had been built nearby. To be near such a school, families
of that particular faith had gradually bought up many of

the homes of the community. It is important to get the facts. It is dangerous to guess.

It is also important to identify the people who are not affiliated with any religious group. These are usually considered prospects for all churches. The best way to get this information is to make a house-to-house canvass. In many communities all denominations join in such an endeavor. Canvassers are enlisted and trained. Assignments are carefully made so that each worker has a reasonable number of homes to visit. Exact information is obtained regarding church affiliation and preference. If a complete survey is not possible or feasible, fairly reliable information may be obtained by spot checks. Make a survey of every fifth or tenth house, or make a survey of a typical section of the community and project the results so as to approximate the whole. Although not completely accurate, the results are more dependable than a guess and can be useful in determining property and building needs.

Economic conditions affect churches. Increasingly, churches are related to economic and industrial conditions. People concentrate where work is favorable and plentiful. They often move when the situation changes. A community with diversified industry is, as a rule, more stable than others. Newer industries give promise of stability. Some progressive companies find it cheaper to move away from worn-out plants than to remodel and modernize them. To know the level of income, the possibility of its continuance, and labor and employment conditions is important to building committees.

Much depends on the vocational types in the community. Is the church trying to reach skilled workers, farmers, laborers, or business and professional constituents? In a growing metropolis, like groups have a tendency to live together in housing developments and neighborhoods that reflect the level of income. Hence the location of a church often tends to limit its ministry to a particular group. To weld together a variety of groups in one congregation is not easy, because of varying interests and backgrounds. Ideally, the gospel of Christ should break down the barriers that restrict fellowship, but in our culture that is not easy.

In larger cities, types of neighborhoods are easily defined. A church program that appeals to one may not appeal to another. Even the types of buildings seem to make a difference. In some communities, an attractive, well-equipped building will be practically empty while nearby a storefront church or rough tabernacle will have a thriving congregation. A wise church will get the facts regarding the community it serves before building. It is too costly to guess.

Homes and families are a chief concern. A church cannot afford to ignore the conditions of the home and the family. As go the families, so will go the churches and the nation. The chief concern must be, not what can the families do to support the church, but what can the church do to strengthen family life and develop Christian homes?

To meet the needs of families, the conditions or situations of families must be known. What is the prevailing type of family life? Are homes owned or rented? Is the family life stable? What is the divorce rate? How many are working mothers? What is the incidence of delinquency and crime? What percentages are churchgoing families? What resources are available for helping families? After getting factual answers to these questions, the church can know much better how to plan to meet the family needs. A community with unstable families could not support a large project. A community with many working mothers may need facilities for a day nursery. Adequate space and equipment may help to combat delinquency and crime. Facilities should be provided to meet the need.

Pastors and committees may not feel inclined to take the time to make such a survey as has been suggested here. In the long run, however, it may be a great time-saver. It is usually possible to go wrong in a hundred directions, but right in only one. A church exists to worship God and to serve people. The church that seeks to live "off" the community will fail, but the one that lives "for" the community will live. This is in accordance with the principle enunciated by Jesus when he said, "Whoever will save his life shall lose it; but whoever shall lose his life for my sake and the gospel's the same shall save it." (Mark 8:35.)

The program of a church will inevitably take the shape of the building. The only wise procedure is to plan the program to meet the needs of the people and then provide facilities that will enable the church to implement the program.

SURVEY THE SITUATION

What is the church doing? How successful is the ministry? To know where it stands, a church must look at itself against the background of needs revealed in a study of the community. The community will affect the church, but the church should also affect the community if it is to be the salt and light of the world as Jesus expected. The strengths and weaknesses must be known. Strengths usually are apparent; weaknesses are not so easily seen. A careful study of the church facilities and activities should point up areas that need attention.

Begin with a study of the membership. How many members are resident and how many are nonresident? How many are active and how many are inactive? Why are the inactive ones not interested? A study of age and sex distribution by graph or population pyramid should reveal strengths and weaknesses of the church's appeal. Compare church growth with the growth of the community. To spot the location of members on the map of the church field should indicate the effectiveness of the church's appeal to people of certain areas.

If the study reveals a large number of unreached people in any particular age group or geographical area, an effort should be made to find out why they are unreached. A good look should be taken at the program and the building and equipment. One church found the answer quickly. The community survey showed a large number of young families with babies and small children. A review of the church records showed very few of these involved in the program. Why? A study of the building gave the clue. One small, dingy, badly equipped basement room was provided for nursery children. Two other rooms in similar condition were available for beginners and primaries. This has been called the "debasement" of the children. Most modern parents will not accept such arrangements for their little ones.

Economic facts about the membership are significant. How many are employed? What is the average income? Does the per capita giving compare favorably with the incomes? Has it increased, or has it decreased, in recent years? Do the changes compare favorably with economic fluctuations of the community as a whole? The giving power and the giving habits of a congregation have a definite bearing on what plans should be made for acquiring physical facilities. A building committee must take a careful look at the giving potential of the congregation.

A church should know its ministries. Very few pastors know exactly how many attend the worship services. It is easy to overestimate. Get the facts! Ushers can count the members present. Such figures kept over a period of years indicate something of the effectiveness of a church's ministry.

It is easy to learn how many people attend the services. Choose a period of four typical Sundays, and register all who attend on these days. Use a sufficient number of small cards with a pencil for each person. Every person present can be registered in the same time it takes for one person to write his name. Another plan is to pass a clipboard holding a registration form down each pew. Church members on each pew can easily spot the visitors and at the close of the service become acquainted with them and help them feel welcome.

Modern churches are building for more than worship services. The organization life of a church must be housed. In former years 80 percent or more of the space was provided for worship. Today, religious education and other activities use from 50 to 80 percent of the floor area. The church program can hardly go beyond what is provided for in its buildings. This fact makes it imperative that future, as well as present, needs be considered in planning. Begin by listing all functions with a clear description of the organizations and the space needs of each. Many parts of the building should be planned for multiple uses.

Growing denominations have an all-age program of religious education. Inclusion of adults in the education program greatly increases the potential numerically, financially, evangelistically, and educationally. To involve adults in small study groups enhances the fellowship. Reach the adults, and the children are sure to attend. Many rapidly growing churches consider the Sunday

School as the agency of the church charged with responsibility of educating, of evangelizing, and of enlisting members.

Many churches provide less than 25 percent of their members with any opportunity to render real Christian service. Nothing would increase the vitality of churches more than to involve a much larger number of adult members in a meaningful service. Christians who serve together, pray together, stay together, and pay together. An all-age Sunday School provides a suitable instrument for such involvement, but it can never be fully realized without an adequate building in which to work.

A careful study should include a chart or table showing growth or decline over a period of years. It should compare attendance with enrollment and membership potential in each organization and department. From the study of population trends, a careful effort should be made to determine how much land and building space the church will need. Remember that a church that expects to grow must allow room for growth. A church usually will get no more than it gets ready for.

There are many good reasons for making a study such as is here suggested. The main concern, however, is to use the information to help in planning a building. It is more important to give attention to why we are building than to what we are building. Mistakes set in concrete and steel can last a long time. They are not easily or cheaply corrected.

A study carefully made should provide answers to important questions, as, for example:

Is the building well located?
Is it adequate for the membership?
Is it attractive and comfortable?

Does it provide well for the services and ministries of the church?

Should additional land be added, or should a new location be sought that will permit growth and a better ministry?

What immediate and long-range objectives should be recommended?

Here are some helpful results that have come from such studies:

1. Many congregations have found a need for establishing new churches or missions to serve people not being reached.
2. A small church in a downtown location found 1,000 prospects within a four-block area which included a large housing project.
3. Some churches have found juvenile delinquency increasing, pointing up a need for more youth activity and recreation.
4. Churches have found that their growth was stifled for lack of parking facilities.
5. One church, after constructing a building, found that the city-operated airport was planning expansion that would cut the church off from one-half of its constituents. With careful study these plans could have been known before the building was erected.
6. Another church found that, if all its members were to come to one worship service, hardly one-fourth could be seated.
7. A church in an established section found that it had nothing in its program that would appeal to an increasing proportion of older people.
8. Still others have found their community filled with young couples and small children. Their great need was improvement and expansion of nursery facilities.
9. Numerous churches have learned that they are poorly

located to serve their constituents because of the distance the members have to drive or because of inadequate parking space.

Following World War II, a study was made of a small suburban church in Houston, Texas. The result was a decision by the church to move from a corner lot to a more adequate site one-fourth mile away. Fifteen years later this church, instead of a small plot and property valued at $40,000, owned eleven acres of ground with buildings and equipment valued at more than $1,500,000. This was begun by a self-study planned and conducted by the laymen of the church.

These are days of rapid change. The investment of large sums of money in church buildings demands that congregations study before they build, lest they build for yesterday instead of tomorrow.

Chapter 3

ACQUIRING THE
BEST LOCATION

THE COMPLETE REPORT of the survey committee should help answer the important question, "Is the church well located?" Possibly the land area should be enlarged by acquiring adjoining property. Is a change of location necessary? Would it be better to enlarge the present site, or to acquire a new one?

The size and location of a site will greatly affect the ability of the church to accomplish its objectives. The best site possible will not be too good. A cheap location may be the most expensive thing a church can have. Churches are usually hard pressed for money, and are tempted to settle for less than the best location. Many churches have been handicapped for a century or more by accepting a gift site. Unless a donated location is where it ought to be, adequate in size, and free of all encumbrances, the church should not accept it unless it is absolutely the only site available. Or, if the donor is willing, the church may accept the gift and sell it or trade for a better location. A large staff, a popular preacher, or even a new building, cannot overcome the handicap of a poor location. When the sign reads "three blocks to Trinity Church," the church should probably be located where the sign is situated.

A large church in a growing Southern city wanted to start a mission in a new subdivision. Three acres in the center of the project was the best site available, but the price was $90,000. This seemed like a costly start for a new work, but the property was purchased. The sponsoring church decided that it would not be an expense but an investment. If the new church served God and the people for a century, the cost of a good location would be less than $1,000 per year. They felt that this was not too much to pay to get a young church well started in its work of reconciling men to God.

A church site should be accessible—to people who need the church, and to people whose support and leadership the church needs. A site near the center of the community is usually preferred. Some conditions, however, may change this preference. A large park, plant, cemetery, airport, or other installation on one side may render the location somewhat inaccessible. A limited-access freeway, a railroad track, or a very busy thoroughfare may interfere with easy access even though the location may be in the geographical center. Since most worshippers come in cars, a location should be sought that is on a route travelled regularly by the largest number of people the church expects to serve. It is easier for people to follow the route normally taken to town, school, or the shopping center.

A church seeking to minister to more than one class of people should try to locate where those constituents who can furnish the church with leadership and financial strength will be reached. It is easier to get the less capable to move upward than vice versa. Some churches have been handicapped for life by starting on a site that discouraged the more capable people of the community from seeking membership.

One church looking for a new location narrowly averted

disaster. A site adequate in size and reasonable in price
was available near a sewage-disposal plant. The prevailing
wind was favorable. Some leaders thought they should
buy it. Fortunately, wise counsel turned them in the direction of another site near a large public school. It was
more expensive, of course, but it was favorably situated to
reach the people who could provide the most help.

A church location should be visible and convenient. A
corner plot is much to be desired. A whole block is better
than one corner. A prestige location is an advantage, provided, of course, that the buildings and improvements
are worth seeing. Safe and convenient access is also important. A location may be within easy reach, be easily
seen, and still not be convenient. A very narrow street, or
a boulevard with fast traffic and limited parking, may increase difficulty and be discouraging to constituents. A
busy street where numbers of men, women, and children
filter through parked cars constitutes a real hazard.

The church location should be favorable for a growing
influence. Past tradition and present circumstances may
be of less importance than future usefulness. Once a large
investment is made in improvements, the chance of changing locations is remote. Good buildings last a long time
and should not be erected until a careful study of population trends is made to determine, if possible, where the
people will be tomorrow.

A large church had served on one of the main business
corners for a century. Extensive improvements were
needed and planned. At the same time an offer of above
$1,000,000 was made for the small but strategic corner
lot. To move or not to move was the question. The center
of the city was gradually shifting to the south. The sale
price would have enabled the church to purchase a block
of ground a few squares away toward the south. It would

also have gone a long way toward providing a new building. The proposed new location would have placed the church where it soon would have been in the heart of this great city for another century. Should the congregation have sold and relocated or should it have remained? To eliminate sentiment would make the answer obvious.

For a church program today and tomorrow, property of adequate size is a must. Numerous city churches, choked to death, could have continued in service if sufficient land had been available for parking and an expanded ministry. Of course, multistory buildings can be erected—but not without extra cost and inconvenience. Such buildings require deep foundations, stairs, elevators, and/or escalators. Construction and maintenance costs increase with the height of buildings. Such installations are not cheap and are not the best for churches. The elimination of stairs and basements is strongly recommended. Older people, the middle-aged, and children have trouble with stairs, and these three groups represent most of the constituents.

A church site should be large enough to permit the adoption of an over-all master plan for buildings. Erecting a plant unit by unit makes financing easier and often enables the church to avoid expensive mistakes. Any church should have at least three acres of land to provide for a membership of three or four hundred. One additional acre is needed for each increase of 300 in membership.

The plot of ground should be large enough to provide parking. Eighty-five to ninety percent of all members go to church by automobile. Since streets are being more and more restricted for parking, and people are increasingly reluctant to walk, parking facilities are a must. Many cities now require churches to provide off-street parking before building permits will be issued. Usually the space requirement is in proportion to the seating capacity of the auditorium. For church parking, it is well to provide at least 300 square feet per car. People go to church in their best clothes and do not like close parking. Adequacy would require one car space for every three in attendance, which in most places is about the average number arriving in each car. An active and appealing church can increase attendance and participation just by enlarging the parking facilities.

Drives to and from parking areas should be clearly marked and easily negotiated. Safety precautions must be taken for pedestrians and passengers. On a busy thoroughfare, space is needed to get cars quickly out of the line of fast traffic. Side and back streets may be used for this purpose to good effect. On the lot, angle parking along one-way drives is helpful. Parking plots near several entrances make for convenience. If the size of the ground will permit, such decentralizing of parking is quite desirable. A paved area that eliminates dust and mud and is attractively marked is inviting to the persons a church hopes to reach. If blacktop is used, it may be well to put reinforced concrete in stopping and unloading zones to prevent wrinkles. Parking lots can be made attractive. Cars parked around the church need not be an ugly sight.

Courteous parking attendants to guide the people are possibly more important than ushers in the sanctuary. Bad public relations resulting from blocked driveways, congested streets, and bent fenders can be avoided through provision of adequate parking arrangements. Not many churches can solve the problem by buying a large parking building as did the First Baptist Church of Dallas, Texas, but they must protect their guests' cars from the vandalism which is rampant in many places. During evening services, a well-lighted parking area is a good deterrent to vandalism; however, patrolling by members of a parking committee may also be required.

To increase the eye appeal, landscaping is important. Building and parking should not cover all the available land space. Walks, drives, suitable shrubs, and trees add greatly to the appeal of a church plant. The more beautiful buildings are not on the property line.

Outdoor areas may be used to good advantage for recreation and education activities. Vacation church-school leaders often use the outdoors for nature studies. Even the paved parking areas can be marked and used for sports such as tennis, volleyball, basketball, and badminton. The church with enough ground and its own softball field makes a strong appeal to boys. Facilities for classes and small groups to have picnics and cookouts on the church grounds are a great asset. Such informal face-to-face group meetings, with opportunity for fellowship, are more effective in changing attitudes than is formal instruction. Lighting that makes possible outdoor activities at night increases the appeal, especially to younger people. Of course, proper supervision is a requirement.

A church should have a level site if possible. A steep hill is hard climbing for those who walk and is bad for parking cars. A site that slopes away from the street offers a street-level entrance to the worship center and provides opportunity for a first floor above ground, which is quite desirable. The width and depth of the land area should be sufficient to permit development of a pleasing master plan.

The site committee, before making a recommendation, must work closely with the study committee. The location of the membership, the present population, the trends, the industries, the railroads, the freeways, the changing religious preferences, and the social and racial patterns should be carefully studied. Facts regarding any or all of these conditions may help determine whether the proposed location is desirable.

Engineering counsel may be needed regarding drainage, danger of flooding, and soil stability. Local codes and ordinances may be controlling factors in such respects as the height of a building, the type of construction, and the location of buildings in regard to property lines. Some courts have held that covenant restrictions apply to churches. Even though such restrictions might have been broken by others in the community, their appearance in the deed puts a cloud on the title and thus may make a mortgage loan difficult.

Once the most suitable location has been agreed upon, the committee should recommend to the church that the land be purchased. If the congregation approves, the site committee (or the legal subcommittee, if it has been appointed) should be instructed to undertake acquisition of the land.

Chapter 4

APPOINTING A
BUILDING COMMITTEE

SINCE A MAJOR expansion effort is a once-in-a-generation undertaking for most churches, great care should be taken in selecting a building committee. The basic purpose of the committee is to get the best thinking of the congregation applied to solving the problem. This suggests the need for a representative committee. A building for God should not be the product of the thinking of a few specialists; it should be a composite of the ideals and aspirations of a purposeful and prayerful congregation.

The size of the committee may depend on the size of the church. The spiritual gains will be in proportion to the number of concerned members who can be meaningfully involved in the project. It is always appropriate for a deliberative congregation to express formally its endorsement of the building committee.

DIVISION OF RESPONSIBILITY

A suitable division of responsibility can best be provided by forming subcommittees. The number and function of the various subcommittees may vary greatly with each situation. A workable list of committees used by many churches is as follows: the worship center committee, education committee, fellowship and recreation committee, committee on administration and other ministries, finance committee, legal committee, construction committee, publicity committee, organ committee, furniture committee, and landscaping committee. The general chairman may appoint a chairman for each subcommittee. With these chairmen, he may form a building council to coordinate the work of the several committees, to make regular progress reports to the congregation, and to consider matters of general concern.

Each subcommittee should have a specific area of responsibility. Careful records should be kept of all meetings. A full written report with recommendations must conclude the work of each group.

PASTOR AND THE BUILDING COMMITTEE

A word of caution may be important for the pastor. Almost never should the pastor be chairman of a building committee. The pastor is the spiritual leader of the congregation and should remain so, especially during the time of building. Members of the committee and the whole congregation will need spiritual strength that his counseling, his preaching, and his praying may bring. The pastor can become so involved in the construction of a church building that he will get blamed for whatever mistakes may occur. The pastor may well be considered an ex officio member of all the committees—to give counsel as he is able. He should remember however, that neither an ordination certificate nor a theological degree automatically qualifies him as an expert in architecture or in construction.

THE BUILDING COMMITTEE
AND THE ARCHITECT

The building committee does not draw the plan for the building. That is the work of the architect but he cannot do his work without the help of the committee. Basically, the committee works out a clear statement of the program needed by every function of the church, specifies the space needs of each organization, and interprets the budget provisions as they relate to the project. The committee helps the architect understand the faith, character, and spirit of the people he seeks to serve. Responsibility for providing an effective building for the congregation rests heavily on the committee as well as on the architect.

TRAINING THE COMMITTEE

Inexperienced people may be of more value on a building committee than experienced ones. They will probably be more teachable and more willing to learn. Laymen serving on a building committee should be trained for their task. A period of intensive study should be planned for the entire committee. Each member of the committee who has a good understanding of the problem will be more cooperative with the group as a whole and more efficient in carrying out a particular function on a subcommittee. It is unfair to give a member a heavy responsibility and not provide the training that will help him meet it.

Of special concern to the whole committee is the report of the study or survey committee. The report, if thoroughly done and adequately evaluated, will answer many questions needed by the plans committee. The pastor may

well lead in such a study, or an outside consultant may be
invited in.

SEEK COUNSEL

There is no excuse for any church building to be inferior or shoddy. More help is available to church building
committees than ever before. Every major denomination
provides guidance for its churches through departments of
church architecture or through building consultants. Some
of them have men trained to give assistance in each state
or ecclesiastical jurisdiction. Most of these departments
have produced excellent materials that are available often
without cost. The National Council of Churches makes
its materials available upon request. Professional consultants, upon invitation, will help a committee survey
the needs and get ready for an architect. Experienced
pastors and education workers can share valuable information. It is economical to prevent mistakes. Help is available. A committee should seek it.

MAKE GOOD USE OF TIME

Once a church decides to build, to be delayed dampens
enthusiasm. But it takes time to plan. The committee
should come to grips with its task quickly but not hur-
riedly. A schedule of meetings should be arranged that
will give each subcommittee time to consider its job. An
occasional joint meeting of all committees provides opportunity for sharing information and for creating a feeling of togetherness. To set at least tentative dates for
completion of various phases of the planning may help to
prevent delay. Plans should not jell too soon, yet unnecessary delay is deadening.

Of course the time schedule will depend on many local

factors. On a very large project, ten to twelve months may be needed for the planning phase and fifteen to eighteen months for construction. On smaller projects, less time will be needed. It is very important to take time to plan well.

A SUGGESTED SCHEDULE

Assuming that the church has accepted the recommendations in the planning and survey report and has authorized a building committee, the following schedule, or a similar one, should be established:

1st month—Building committee selected and organized into subcommittees with chairman and secretary for each. Architect selected if he has not already been chosen.

2nd month—Intensive study by whole committee of planning and building procedures, each subcommittee carefully defining its own function.

3rd, 4th, and 5th months—Planning subcommittees define space needs of each function and work with architect in developing sketches that will coordinate all needs. When a suitable floor plan is agreed upon, the church should approve.

6th, 7th, and 8th months—Architect and his engineers complete detailed drawings with specifications, looking toward bids from contractors. Church considers plans and approves them if acceptable.

9th month—Plans put out for bids; contract let; ground-breaking services held.

10th month—Construction begins.

20th month—Construction completed; building inspected and accepted.

21st month—Building furnished, occupied, and dedicated.

CRITERIA

At the outset of the work of the building committee, considerable attention should be given to the matter of criteria. What basic qualities should be held and what definite goals set? Over-all objectives that will guide many choices should be determined. Too many church buildings are erected in spurts, with a disconnected unit added every now and then according to the whims of the present leadership. Too often the concern is for space only. How much area in square feet should be provided? Too little attention has been given to qualitative values. An old but true saying is "If you aim at nothing, you will hit it every time." Let the committee struggle with the problem of ideals. If clear objectives are set and an earnest effort made to reach them, much can be done to achieve usefulness, unity, flexibility, and beauty. Yes, a good building should do even more; it should convey religious truth that strengthens its witness.

UTILITY

First and foremost, the building should have utility. It should be functional in the sense that it is useful. It must be designed to accommodate well the numbers of people who will use it. The circulation must be right. It should be comfortable, durable, and efficient. Too many people are concerned from the first about appearance of the building or its style of architecture. Often a functional building is equated with modern architecture. But a building that is functional means a building that is practical. It is built to serve. Even the traditional types of architecture were built to serve their day, hence were functional. Any well-planned building can be adorned or dressed in a suitable and pleasing way. Give attention first to its function. If the structure does not take care of the program, whatever beauty it has will be wasted.

UNITY

A church plant should have unity. It should be planned to fit the site and give the impression of completeness. The various units should fit together. They should preferably be parts of one building. The campus type of church plant with units apart and well located on spacious grounds makes a beautiful appearance, but it can hardly escape giving some impression of fragmentation. The church is one body, and all parts of it should be so related as to say, "We are not divided." Worship, teaching, and administration are but separate functions working to achieve the same goal. Different age groups sometimes come into conflict. Let us not suggest or encourage such division by the design of our buildings. Besides, in foul weather, movement from one building to another is difficult. The unity referred to here gives the plant a balanced and a finished look that speaks of stability and permanence, as well as oneness. A building for God's use should exemplify the qualities of character that are so much a part of His nature.

FLEXIBILITY

A modern church has a variety of functions. Many rooms have to be shared by various groups using them at different times. All such possibilities should be carefully studied so as not to overbuild and incur undue expense. No church is justified in building more than it actually needs. One cause of great concern is that so much money is put into expensive church buildings to be used for such a limited time each week. Special effort should be made to build with a flexibility that will ensure maximum return on the investment.

The type of construction may contribute to the ideal of flexibility. A good building is designed to permit changes in the program. Education and liturgy are not static; they change constantly. Because of population shifts, age groupings may need to be altered radically within one generation. What is known as a young people's church today will not remain so always. It is wise then to eliminate load-bearing walls, so that partitions can be moved. Movable cabinets may add to the flexibility.

BEAUTY

A building committee should strive for more than utility, unity, and flexibility. Beauty should also be sought. The beauty connected with the worship of God may be very simple, rather than ornate or pretentious. Was the church in New York that spent $850,000 to give its front entrance what the architect called "a Fifth Avenue look" trying to achieve beauty as an aid to worship, or was there another motive? Would not beauty of another type be more becoming to a church in a day of great human suffering and need?

There is a type of beauty closely allied with simplicity and integrity. A church building that fits its site and opportunity, avoiding imitation and sham, can be beautiful without being pretentious. Architects and building committees should not yield to the temptation to be novel and clever, or to resort to gimmicks, but should stay with those attributes of beauty that last and that truly represent the Christian spirit.

TRUTH

A church building should give more than utility and beauty. It should teach. Its design and arrangement should convey the truth that undergirds worship and every function of the church in its ministry.[1] Church buildings should convey, in design and material, the congregation's concept of what God is like. He is creator, therefore powerful, majestic, and awesome. He is judge of the earth yet is a friend and is loving. He is transcendent and yet always with us. How can some of these truths be translated into brick and stone? Obviously, it is not easy. God is too great to be properly portrayed in any symbol. To magnify unduly the "otherness" of God may result in an atmosphere of cold austerity. To magnify unduly the "immanence" of God may lead into the "homey," "clubby" type of warmth that sometimes gives the impression that the Almighty is a wonderful chum. Just what is the answer? No one has found it completely, but we must keep trying to design church buildings that will express our beliefs. Every building committee, with earnest prayer and the help of an architect, should seek the course that will enable the church to fulfill its mission.

Many church planners feel that a building should say something about the nature of the Church as it is understood by the congregation. If the Church is conceived as an army of God, why not house it in a long narrow building that gives the impression of a procession? If it is viewed as an assembly of passive people being ministered to by professional leaders or performers, why not a theatrical arrangement? When the Church is seen primarily as a

[1] For an excellent discussion on this subject see "Fundamentals for Church Builders," *Your Church*, April, 1961, EA Sovik-AIA.

proclaimer of a message, why not an auditorium with appointments suitable for public speaking? Some have magnified the Church as the school of Christ and are quite interested in the educational aspects of the church's ministry. Still others insist that the Church is the body of Christ, or the active agency of the Kingdom, continuing to do in our day the work that Christ did while he was in his human body. Each of these images, and many more, have Biblical bases, but it is hardly possible—and certainly not desirable—that all of these notions could be stressed in any one building.

One image that is getting considerable attention is that of the Church as the family of God. God's presence is among his people. Jesus promised to be where two or three are gathered together. God is our Father. Christians are brothers and sisters. This image was used repeatedly by early Christian writers. The stresses, conflicts, and division of modern days seem to suggest that it may have great usefulness for us today. Possibly it would contribute to the revival of concern by the laity and enhance the timely emphasis on the great doctrine of the priesthood of all believers. Any such emphasis may well be encouraged with the hope that, increasingly, the whole congregation may be better equipped for ministry.

Can such a concept be conveyed in architecture? Many attempts are being made to achieve it. The long narrow nave would not do. More width for the place of worship would be needed to give the feeling of being close together around a table. Sloping floors are too much like a theater. Suggestions have been made to make the choir a part of the congregation with all seated somewhat circularly around the table. Sermons, readings, prayers, and other parts of the service may originate from various places. This would call for several focal points rather than one, but it may give a fellowship more of a feeling of participating rather than just listening or observing. Here again it seems that a committee that really cares will struggle with these questions in order to come out with what it feels God wants for that church.

A word of warning is that there is no magic in symbols. They cannot be expected to bring in the Kingdom. The New Testament Christians had no church buildings at all but did pretty well. In Europe, many churches gained fame through their architecture but lost their congregations. In spreading the gospel, God has chosen to work through a redeemed and dedicated fellowship of people—His family. For this there is no substitute.

IMPORTANT DECISIONS ABOUT CONSTRUCTION

The building committee must select a method of construction. Churches are built in a number of different ways. Local conditions have to be considered in making the choice.

Probably the most common way, and in many respects the most satisfactory, is to have a general contract. Usually this is a turn-key job. One contractor is responsible for everything. The price of the contract covers the entire cost of the building. The general contract offers several advantages to the church, for example:

1. The exact cost of the building can be known in advance. The finance committee can negotiate for a definite amount of money on a long-term loan or on a construction or interim loan.
2. Often a savings may be realized by receiving competitive bids from competent contractors. A good contractor knows well what his organization and his subcontractors

can do and at what price; he will bid accordingly. A contractor's profit usually is figured on a percent of the cost of the job.

3. A better job will usually result when a reputable contractor with a competent crew, under the supervision of a good architect, has complete charge of the project.

4. The work of supervision is easier. If replacement of inferior work or correction of minor mistakes would mean additional cost to the church, the architect will hesitate to order it. But if such adjustments are included in the contract, there is no question; the architect will require the contractor to make the contract good.

5. When one firm is responsible for carrying the work through to completion, the building committee and the pastor are relieved of many minor details.

6. The building the church buys can be guaranteed. A reputable contractor can provide a performance bond that assures the church of the completion of the building. Even if the contractor's company should fail, the bonding company will complete the building according to plans and specifications set forth in the contract.

A church may serve as its own contractor. Usually someone experienced in construction work must do the work of a contractor in coordinating and supervising. A church following this plan usually employs a superintendent or obtains volunteer services of one of its members who is qualified and willing to assume the responsibility. Churches that use this method may be able to take advantage of customary discounts on materials and to make use of skilled workers in the congregation. The Reverend A. H. McEachern, pastor of Westmoreland Baptist Church, Huntington, West Virginia, described such an undertaking as follows:

In 1961, we constructed an educational building with 12,000 square feet. The architectural department of our denomination submitted preliminary drawings. A local architect drew the plans but did not supervise construction. A contractor who is a member of the church supervised construction—gratis. About sixty men in the church gave volunteer labor according to their skills. We did not hire a carpenter until after the roof was on. Some contracts were sublet—bricklaying and roofing. The church purchased all materials, saving three percent sales tax and receiving contractors kickbacks. We hired a plumber for installation of eighteen toilets and the air-conditioning units. We hired men to install furnace and air-conditioning duct work with the church furnishing materials. All electrical work was done on a volunteer basis. We had no disagreements or serious problems in the process. We constructed a building valued at $120,000. We put new equipment throughout, including offices and choir room (which are carpeted and panelled). We bought five pianos and installed 22 tons of air conditioning for $65,000 total cost.

This pastor said, "The key is good supervision. It is not the easy way to build. It took a great deal of the pastor's time, but resulted in a deeper fellowship in the church. It saved a considerable amount of money and it involved a good number of skilled men in meaningful work for the Lord."

There are dangers. If the method were unsuccessful for any reason, it would be difficult and expensive to get a contractor to finish the job. Securing a loan may be difficult because there is no certainty as to what the cost will be. A common fault is for a committee to underestimate the cost in such a method. If this occurs, the changes that must be made in the plans or the quality of materials may greatly reduce the usefulness of the facilities. In this type of construction, the church must take the risks that the general contractor would normally take. Sometimes these are considerable and dangerous. There is also the possibility that no significant savings will be realized. General contractors buy all materials at the most favorable prices, which may just about match what the church would get in discounts. It is also true that subcontractors depend almost wholly on general contracts for their work. When they do close bidding and good work, they get more jobs. Whether the usual church discounts would be more advantageous is open to question.

The "cost-plus" method is sometimes used. The contractor's fee is a percentage of the cost of the building. In times of uncertainty this may be a good method to use. A contractor in making a firm bid must include in his price every possible contingency. If there is a chance that more favorable conditions would occur during construction, money may be saved. Great care must be taken, however, to get a builder who has unusual competence and integrity. When the builder's fee is based on the amount of money he spends, there is not much incentive for economy. With poor management and unfavorable conditions, the costs could become unbearable.

A variation of this plan is that of providing a fixed fee for the contractor, thus removing the incentive for large spending.

The "cost-plus" method seems to be more applicable to projects whose cost cannot be figured in advance. Extensive remodeling of an old building is an example.

Many churches have been built entirely by volunteer labor. Small new churches that have no established credit and can raise only limited funds often successfully construct their own buildings. The First Church of God, Fresno, California, used 10,000 hours of volunteer labor in such a project. An interesting account of this effort may be found in *Church Management* magazine, January 1962.

Here again, the quality of work done and the satisfaction received by the members depend a great deal upon the kind of supervision provided.

SELECTION OF MATERIALS

Another important decision is that of selecting the materials to be used. Of course, the advice of the architect will usually be taken because he is the expert. However, architects are usually open to suggestions from members of the building committee who are informed on the strengths and weaknesses of the materials. New materials offer a variety never before available. Some make possible new designs that should be considered. Others provide opportunity for economy in construction. An illustration is found in the widespread use of blocks instead of lath and plaster for walls. Some builders claim that glass walls can be installed more cheaply than others.

Good choice of low-maintenance materials is a means of great economy, since maintenance is always a big item in the operating budget. It is good procedure to consult experienced maintenance men before building. The building design, the type of construction, and the choice of materials may help or hinder property maintenance.

Savings can be made by standardizing various component parts of the building, such as windows, doors, and toilet facilities. For corridors, glazed tile, instead of plaster, is less easily marred; wall-hung fixtures are easier to install. Recessed floor mats at entrances catch dirt and prevent it from spreading. Fiber glass drapes do not have to be flameproofed to meet fire regulations. Colored glass may eliminate the need for drapes. Stainless steel and aluminum require less care than ornamental brass. Service to lights in high ceilings is facilitated by providing attic space. In some areas, carpets are cheaper in the long run than the cheapest of floor tile. As far as possible, avoid the use of wood where it must be exposed to the weather. These few suggestions will indicate that serious attention should be given to built-in maintenance.

THE UNIT PLAN

An important early decision must be made in regard to a master plan. Fortunate is the congregation that has resources to build a complete plant at one time. Not many churches are so affluent. With the help of the architect, the committee must develop a total plot scheme before floor plans are drawn. This plot plan will locate on the site all present buildings or units and all others anticipated even in the distant future. Such an overview may point up a need for more land. If such is the case, more land should be acquired, if at all possible, before plans are finalized. It is quite risky for a church to plan for the future use of real estate that it does not own, unless binding agreement for future transfer of the land has been signed. If the site is ample, those responsible for planning must know the relationships of the various units. The congregation also should be encouraged to see what its dream will look like when it becomes a reality.

When a church cannot build a complete plant, the total plot plan is more important. It will provide space for the first units and will give assurance that adequate space will be available when later units can be added.

"Which unit should be built first?" is an important question. Here there are several opinions. Much depends on the strategy of the church in meeting the needs of its constituents. Every congregation should adopt the approach that seems most likely to help it succeed in fulfilling its mission.

Many churchmen would immediately say, "Build the

sanctuary first." J. R. Scotford says that the best approach is to build for worship. "Religious commitments are what builds a church." [2] He would make the worship approach primary because, he says, this is what people want and what they will more readily pay for. Here again it depends upon what the church is trying to do. If the main objective is to minister to a congregation already trained in worship, no doubt this is the best approach. However, if the opportunity for evangelism is great, an approach that includes a strong emphasis on Bible study and fellowship may be more effective.

To build for worship appeals strongly to many, but some problems are involved. Usually the worship center costs more money than other units. Considerable resources are required to build the permanent worship center. A building erected for the worship of God should be a good one. If a church is growing, it is hard to tell what size the worship center should be. Properly constructed worship centers are difficult and costly to enlarge. It may be wiser to wait until a church achieves its growth. Some planners have also made the point that the building for worship should come as a climax to a progressive undertaking.

An article by Bernard W. Guenther suggests that a good solution is to build a shell sufficiently large to take care of needs, present and future, and then finish it at a later time.[3] "Put your investment in space," the author says. Space is expensive, however, and to be useful, it has to be furnished, heated, cooled, and maintained. This is probably not a good solution for many churches.

Large numbers of churches have found it more helpful to build one or more education units first. Particularly will

[2] Scotford, J. R., *When You Build Your Church* (New York: Channel Press, 1958), p. 47.

[3] Bernard W. Guenther, "Build First the Shell" *Church Management* Jan. 1962, p. 21.

a young church with limited finances and considerable potential find this a suitable plan. Worship need not be neglected. Churches of various sizes can plan ample space, with appointments that are quite conducive to worship, on the first floor of an education unit. This type of construction is much less expensive.

For churches planning to use volunteer labor, as many do in getting started, a simple type of building is most suitable. All the various functions of a church can be maintained fairly well in such a building, whereas it would be much more difficult to do this in the worship center. When the time comes for enlargement, this type of space is flexible and easily adapted for various uses.

If the opportunity and mission of the church calls for the evangelistic approach to winning unreached people to Christ, the church should consider putting the emphasis on enlistment in Bible study and small-group fellowship as well as in worship. This calls for education space.

HOW ABOUT BASEMENTS?

The committee must decide whether to have a basement. Most churches have a basement, usually under the worship center. Such construction is no longer necessary nor desirable. Why should anyone dig a hole in the ground and then put a church building into it—unless there is extreme scarcity of ground? Apply the cost of excavation to acquisition of adjoining land and put the building above ground where there is light and air. In the long run it is cheaper and much more desirable. W. A. Harrell, Church Architecture Department, Southern Baptist Sunday School Board, Nashville, Tennessee, has compiled a list of objections to church basements. An adaptation of the list is used here with his permission.

CHURCH BASEMENTS ARE NOT PRACTICAL

A basement is that portion of a building with the floor level below grade to the extent that it requires areaways or light shafts to provide adequate windows, and/or doorways on two or more sides. A ground or first floor obtained when building on a sloping lot, with three sides out of the ground, is not a basement.

1. *Basements are not economical.* Contrary to opinion, a basement is not economical. On a contractual basis, the cost of floor space thus situated in a building is more expensive than the cost of the same area constructed at grade level. Basements located under sanctuaries usually increase construction cost of this unit of the building.

2. *Basements are psychologically poor.* Psychologically, a basement arrangement produces a negative effect upon a church congregation. Many churches have constructed them as a first unit of church buildings, with a temporary roof, hoping to add other stories very soon, only to be disappointed by having to use this area for years in its unfinished state. Moreover, the pattern established in some first units of this type has, when the superstructure was to have been added, proved too small and far from structurally adequate.

3. *Basements are often left unfinished.* In many instances this type of space, unfinished on the inside with the idea that it will be finished later, is used ten to fifteen years before further finishing is done.

4. *Basements increase steps.* Access to sanctuaries over basements usually necessitates excessive steps. This is objectionable, especially to aged and physically handicapped people attending worship services.

5. *Basement construction often penalizes space.* Because of construction considerations, a basement must have

columns and other undesirable features that handicap activities to be housed in that area.

6. *Religious educators discourage basements.* Recognized authorities on religious education are opposed to basements for education purposes.

7. *Public schools are discontinuing basements.* Modern buildings for public schools usually have no basements. Since much activity in religious education is similar to that of weekday education, we should evaluate housing facilities of the latter.

8. *Building codes may prohibit basements.* Some communities prohibit construction of basement space for occupancy and use by large numbers of people.

9. *Multistory structures are not desirable.* Generally, church builders are avoiding multiple-story construction when ample property is available. When a basement is added to a one-story building, it becomes multistory. Two or more stairways are required in multistory buildings. Additional space must be constructed to allow for these stairways, or space to accommodate people must be sacrificed.

10. *Unsavory odors linger in basements.* In some sections of the country, it is impossible to construct basement space that will not be affected by unsavory odors.

11. *Planners seldom occupy basement space.* Basement areas usually are planned and constructed by persons who do not expect to occupy them.

12. *Basement space is mentally depressing.* Some people object to using a basement room because it gives them a feeling of depression.

13. *Basements are difficult to heat.* Without elaborate and expensive equipment installations, heating a basement often presents a real problem.

14. *Overhead space is often unsightly.* Heating and air-conditioning ducts, plumbing pipes, and the like, suspended overhead, are unsightly.

15. *Modern heating does not require basement space.* No longer is it necessary to have a basement for heating and air-conditioning mechanisms.

16. *Basements require undersized windows.* Installation of full-sized windows in a basement is usually out of the question. Younger children often are housed in basements where not even a casual observation can be made of nature when the leader speaks of God's beautiful world.

17. *Basement space is not recognized as "God's house."* Children have difficulty in respecting a basement as being a part of God's house. They associate basement space and recreation, since such areas in homes and public buildings are equipped for this purpose.

18. *Basements are often damp.* To avoid basement dampness, and even flooding, during wet-weather seasons usually increases construction costs.

19. *Basement space is a maintenance problem.* Basement areas require more frequent cleaning, repairing, and redecoration.

20. *Money spent in a basement becomes "hidden talents."* Why should we spend God's money to provide beautiful and attractive buildings, and then bury a large percentage of it below grade where it cannot be seen and appreciated? "But he that had received one talent went and digged in the earth, and hid his Lord's money" (Matt. 25:18).

ONE FLOOR OR MORE

"Should churches build multistory buildings?" is a question worthy of consideration. The trend is definitely toward a one-floor plan, and for several good reasons. Low units well placed on an adequate plot of ground can be made very beautiful. In a setting where there are trees and suitable shrubbery, such construction is pleasing and inviting, avoiding the institutional look.

A chief objection to multistory churches is the necessity of climbing stairs. Most churchgoers are older people and children, and might well be protected from the stair-climbing inconvenience. Two elderly people said recently: "We love our church but cannot attend because our heart condition will not permit us to climb stairs." Even young people and their middle-aged parents do not rejoice at the opportunity of mounting a stairway.

A more usual argument against multistory buildings is that they are more expensive. Use of modern materials and construction methods, many builders maintain, renders a one-floor plan less expensive. The foundation can be cheaper. Slab floors and simple walls add to the savings. Space is saved in stairwells and corridors. The safety features of one-story buildings are valuable. Moreover, the one-story building can provide direct access from the outside to departments. Extending or adding to a one-story building is much easier. Considerable savings accrue because ground-floor buildings are cheaper to build and to maintain. If the site is adequate, a one-story building may be best.

Chapter 5

PLANNING THE BUILDING

THE BIGGEST and most important job of the building committee is to develop plans that are adequate for the various functions of the church. This is such a heavy task that it must be shared with a number of people. Having a small plans committee might get the work done effectively but would leave out an important group of people who should be involved. The plans committee should include the most dedicated and the most imaginative members of the congregation.

A good way to approach the problem is to have four separate subcommittees share the responsibility. One group should study the special needs of the worship center and work with the architect to make the plans. This unit is sometimes called the "auditorium" or the "sanctuary," but for purposes of this book the term *worship center* will be used.

Another group should study the needs of the education organizations. Of course, everything a church does is in some measure educational—and learning that comes through informal experience and association is often more effective and lasting than any other. Almost every church, however, has a program of formal education that must be housed. The most loyal and effective workers should be responsible for planning to meet the education needs.

An increasingly important function of many churches is to provide recreation and fellowship for congregations that are becoming both younger and older. A special committee is needed to give this function proper attention. Other committees may be so deeply involved otherwise that this aspect of church life may not receive the consideration it deserves. Fellowship and social activity, guided in a Christian way, can be a means of spiritual growth.

A fourth committee should be responsible for planning the office space and that needed by other administrative services so important to modern churches. So many functions are planned in, and operated from, this area that its importance can hardly be overemphasized.

These four committees must coordinate their work carefully. This may call for extra effort on the part of the chairmen of subcommittees as they work together and with the architect. Too much independence might find each group planning for more space than would be needed in view of the fact that many rooms can be used for more than one function. Each committee, however, should lay out ideal plans and make recommendations that will achieve the highest efficiency. Plans can be cut back, or functions coordinated, more easily than they can be enlarged. Multiple uses of various rooms can be agreed upon in the process of coordinating. Aiming low is more of a mistake than eventually settling for less than the ideal.

These four groups will develop in writing a complete program statement of all the functions of the church, clearly defining the space needed for each department and the interrelatedness of the various activities. Then they will work together and with the architect to provide for every one of the needs in the floor plans that he must produce.

PLANNING THE WORSHIP CENTER

No greater commission could be given to any part of the building committee than to plan the worship center. Making this unit inspiring, inviting, beautiful, comfortable, and effective will require prayerful study and planning. Such a building should support the theological beliefs of the congregation as well as provide ample space for people to worship. It should say to those who view it, "Man shall not live by bread alone," and should reflect and measure the devotion and dedication of those who build it. The increasing emphasis on the importance of worship should encourage the committee to make the greatest effort possible. With such an opportunity, the committee should restudy traditional procedures with a view to improvement and should include in the new plans the items necessary to effect such improvement.

LOCATION

The location of the worship center on the site should be one of prominence. If a church building occupies a whole block, a center spot with education units on both sides gives a good balance. It also gives convenient access to worshippers coming from the education buildings. In many cases, the corner will provide the most conspicious and pleasing location. Since worship is of greatest importance, the worship center should be in a prominent position. There is almost complete agreement that a steeple, pylon, bell cove, or free-standing tower should be erected to give the worship center additional distinctiveness.

ENTRANCE

The entrance to a place of worship should be inviting, but in some churches it is foreboding. If at all possible, it should have not more than one or two steps. Too many worshippers in Protestant churches have to mount a huge pile of concrete in order to make it into the church building. They are glad to hear an usher say, "May I show you to a seat?" No one will ever know how many would-be worshippers have passed by because of the steps. Fewer steps are more important now than ever before because of the increasing number of older people. A concerned church will also provide a ramp at one end of the entrance, and possibly an elevator for cripples and for those in wheelchairs. Where steps are essential, a handrail in the center or at both ends should be included. The approach to the entrance should be well lighted and easily recognized.

The doors are important. J. R. Scotford says, "The door is to a church what a bull's-eye is to a target. It is the spot where people want to come." [1] Tall, thick, oak doors, strengthened with heavy bands of brass, could remind one of a fortress. They may be given a more inviting look. Department stores apparently feel that glass is the most inviting kind of entrance. Churches might do well to follow the example. A look at what is inside may arouse interest and curiosity. Many people rebel, however, at anything so close to commercialism. Wooden doors can be made attractive. A bright, clean, well-painted, and well-kept wooden door does attract attention and will suggest to many that they enter.

Entrances should be conveniently located, preferably facing the principal street at the front of the building. One

[1] J. R. Scotford, *Op. cit.*, p. 42.

large church in Texas, however, with a spacious parking area, has faced its worship center toward that direction with good effect. Doors should swing to the outside and be equipped with panic bars and kick plates. Church entrances and doors should be readily identifiable and inviting so as to make it easy for all to enter.

NARTHEX

The narthex or the vestibule is the first room one sees as he enters to worship. It should be on the same level as the nave. Seldom do new buildings provide a small narrow vestibule. Ample size and depth contribute greatly to the fellowship as well as provide adequate space for those waiting to be ushered in. In inclement weather, worshippers should be able to put on topcoats without being pushed into the snow by those who sat nearer the front. The welcoming committee is usually happy to have the narthex extend across the entire front of the building. There is something about a roomy place that says, "You are really welcome. There is room for you." To convey warmth, a table with flowers and a place to register are needed.

To prepare well for worship, people need to feel quickly that they are entering the house of God. A silence sign is a bit brash as well as ineffective. A loudspeaker in the vestibule will let those entering know what is happening. It is embarrassing for latecomers and disturbing to others to open the door during the invocation or the reading of the scripture. One church considers installation of a glass wall partition between the narthex and the nave to be an effective solution. According to a leader of that church, "When a worshipper steps into the narthex and views the sanctuary, quietness and an attitude of reverence are instantaneous."

For the convenience of all who enter, adequate space for wraps should be provided. This may be done by installing hat and coat racks along a wall. Or probably a better way would be to provide an adjoining room that can be locked. Vandals have been known to rush into churches and steal a number of wraps.

Some of the newer churches have a bride's room. Provided with suitable furniture and equipment for dressing, this room is of great convenience for weddings. The entrance should be in the vestibule.

One church is pleased to show a large and well-equipped church parlor at one end of the vestibule. It serves well as a place for early comers to wait and provides an ideal arrangement for pastor and church leaders to meet informally with visitors and new people after worship services.

NAVE

The nave is the area where worshippers gather. A level floor is preferable to a sloping floor and is generally considered to be more worshipful. A sloping floor gives more of a theatrical atmosphere, and a worshipping congregation is not just an audience to be entertained. A level floor is less expensive to build. To avoid interruption of vision, the platform need be raised only slightly to accomplish all the advantages of the sloped floor. To completely clear the vision for each row of worshippers would require a floor slope too steep to be practical. The room should be rectangular. "The desirable proportion pattern is two-four-five—two for height, four for width, and five for length." [2]

[2] W. A. Harrell, *Planning Better Church Buildings* (Nashville: Convention Press, 1957), p. 18.

SEATING

Almost everyone is agreed that pews offer the best seating arrangement. The modern type of pew with individual arm rests is less preferable, especially under crowded conditions, because it reduces considerably the number of people that can be seated. Individual seats with pew ends and backs are comfortable and attractive but have the same limitation. Opera chairs are comfortable but expensive and not very "churchy." Pews must be custom made and should harmonize with the color scheme and architectural design of the worship center. The contract for pews must be let early, for delivery in time for the dedication or consecration of the building.

The average space between pews is two feet ten inches, back to back. The length of the pews is determined by the size of the room, the number of aisles desired, and the local building code (which may limit the maximum length). Calculations indicate that seating space on pews requires eighteen inches per person. In the nave, seating space requires seven square feet per person if straight pews are used, and about eight square feet if the pews are circular. This figure allows for aisles, the platform, and other necessary space.

AISLES

Aisles should extend the length of the room. Blind aisles that open only part of the way are confusing and deceptive. The main aisle or aisles should be four or five feet wide; secondary ones, two and a half or three feet. Whether a church has a center aisle depends much on the church's tradition and its theology and use of symbolism. Many Protestant churches prefer a center aisle because it gives a place of prominence to the symbols in the center of the church. The center aisle is also more popular for weddings.

BALCONY

Should a church plan for a balcony? The answer is that not all churches need a balcony. Many churches with three hundred or less in attendance will do better without a balcony. For churches with from three hundred to nine hundred worshippers, a balcony across the back of the nave should be adequate. Large churches may need a balcony across the back and down the sides. Almost every church needs additional seating space on certain occasions. When not in use, balconies do not seem to be a great hindrance. When they are not needed, it is a simple matter to close the stairways with a gate, a light chain, or an ornamental rope. Special care should be taken in planning the tiers in the side balconies to make sure that all worshippers have a view of the platform.

CHANCEL

The front portion of the worship center is called the chancel. This is the area in which the ministers and the musicians function in their role as leaders of worship. The chancel furnishings and equipment to be provided include the platform, pulpit, lectern, communion table, baptistry or font, the symbols, the choir loft, and the instruments. Opinions differ considerably concerning arrangement of the chancel.

There seems to be a trend in the direction of the divided chancel. In this arrangement, the communion table with the Bible, and such symbols as are used, are at the back of and in the center of the chancel. With a center aisle, entering worshippers have a straight view to these symbols. On one end of the platform is the pulpit, from which the sermon is delivered. At the other end is the lectern, where the scripture lessons are read. The choir is sometimes divided, a part on each side, or the organ may be on one side and the choir on the other.

Those who favor the divided chancel see as one advantage the fact that the communion table and the symbols are given a place of prominence. Another advantage claimed for this arrangement is that of balance given by putting the pulpit and organ on one side and the choir and lectern on the other. A third reason offered for the divided chancel is that it gives a less conspicuous place to the minister and keeps him from dominating the worship service.

Those who look with disfavor on the divided chancel can argue strongly for the central pulpit. The communion table, more in the center of the room in front of the pulpit, is nearer the center and closer to more of the worshippers. The open Bible on a stand and God's messenger speaking from it are nearer to the genius of evangelical churches, they say. Those who view the church primarily as an evangelizing agency will not easily be swayed from this position.

Many Christians claim that a place of worship divided into a nave and a chancel tends to classify people into two categories—the clergy and the laity. They hold to the opinion that emphasis on the symbols gives the impression that God's presence is more definitely in one place than in another. They remind us that this arrangement was not used in early Christianity and that many of the early Protestants rejected it as being in conflict with the doctrine of the priesthood of all believers.

Of course, one thing this discussion says is that there is no "approved" plan. Churches of all denominations have used well a variety of arrangements. Each church should study its own faith and mission and then decide, under God, what is the best for that particular church.

The platform should be approximately 18 inches in height for rooms 40 to 50 feet long. Twenty-four inches is probably sufficient for rooms sixty to seventy feet long. The depth is even more important. Six feet six inches is considered a minimum, and the length should be at least twelve feet. Steps should lead from the platform down to the floor of the nave. Many larger churches with central pulpits that require higher platforms have tiers of steps the whole length of the platform. This seems to help unify the space by making the rise from nave to chancel gradual, thereby giving the impression that the worship center is really one room and not two separate compartments.

The growing emphasis on the church as the family of God is encouraging experiments with the location of the baptistry, the altar, and the communion table. Can the table be so located as to give the impression that the congregation is seated around it? Some unique attempts have been made to produce this effect.[3] If this can be achieved, many will rejoice. In the meantime, a simple but beautiful table located as near the center of the room as is practicable will suffice for most churches. The spirit of the congregation and the depth of commitment of the worshipper, however, are more important than the physical aspect of symbolism.

For those who baptize by aspersion, the font could be located nearer the center, with all the congregation some-

[3] For a detailed discussion, and photographs, see *How to Get Your Church Built*, by C. Harry Atkinson, published by Doubleday & Company, Inc., Garden City, N.Y. (1964).

what in a circle saying "Welcome" to the new member. Baptists, and others who practice immersion for baptism, usually build the baptistry in the center of the chancel at the back and above the choir. Other procedures are used to welcome and assimilate new members into the fellowship.

INSTRUMENTS AND CHOIRS

In planning the worship center, provision must be made for musical instruments. If only the organ is to be used, the console is sometimes placed in the center of the platform in front of the choir. This may be quite desirable if the organist is the music director. In a divided-chancel arrangement, the organ usually is placed on one side opposite the choir. Where a piano and organ are used together, provision might be made for one at each end of the platform on each side of the speaker's stand. The instruments may rest on the floor of the nave or be slightly raised, but they should not be at the same height as the speaker's platform. This projects the instrumentalists into unnecessary prominence.

Organ chambers should be located above the choir and be opened so that choir members as well as the congregation may hear every tone of the organ. The organ committee should be consulted regarding the proper amount of space to be allowed for the organ.

The location of the choir may be determined by the congregation's concept of the basic purpose of choirs. If the purpose of a choir is to prepare and deliver beautiful music as praise to God, *for the congregation,* it may be located in the front, in the transept, or in the rear balcony, as some have suggested. But if the primary purpose of the choir is to *lead the congregation* in the singing of hymns and gospel songs, as many affirm, it should be located on the platform, behind the pulpit, and facing the congregation.

To plan well for choir space, a church must decide what kind of music program is anticipated. A small professional choir needs a minimum of space. A church that desires an adult choir, and possibly a youth choir, needs a greater amount of choir space. A program of music that includes multiple choirs is increasing in popularity, however. Many churches have six or eight choirs. But it is not always necessary to provide separate choir space in the worship center for all these groups. Seldom do all of them serve at the same time. By using the transepts, the front parts of the balcony, and the front seats of the nave, special music programs using several choirs can be arranged.

Very large churches may wish to seat all the choirs in the chancel. If so, the adult choir may be situated in the center. Space for other choirs of varying ages may be located on each side. Such an arrangement requires very careful planning and placement of choirs, instruments, and pulpit. Plans for an enlarged music program should provide for robing rooms, a practice room, and a music library. If these facilities are in the worship center, they should be in additional rooms behind the chancel. These accoutrements may be in the education area if it is adjacent to the worship center.

VENTILATION

More sermons have been ruined and more worship services deadened by foul and stuffy air than by any other force. In this scientific era there is no excuse for poor ventilation. A simple, inexpensive device called a thermostat can regulate the heat in any room. There is no longer any need for anyone to revive a lagging fire in a potbelly stove in order to produce needed warmth, nor for anyone to open the windows for a period of cooling and fresh air.

The heating problem is less bothersome nowadays, but many churches still have not appropriated the blessings of summer air conditioning. Cooling in the summer is just as needful for millions of people as is heating in the winter. It would help many churches to continue an active program through the summer. The summer slump need not be taken for granted. Air conditioning may be considered an investment rather than an expense, for in most cases it would increase interest and participation and tend to offset the cost. Not only would services be more effective, but deterioration of furnishings would be reduced, and screens, insects, and outside noises would be eliminated. Efficient systems that use the same mechanical equipment for both heating and cooling can be installed. When planning to build, look carefully into the matter of complete air conditioning.

WINDOWS

With complete air conditioning, windows are not absolutely necessary for either light or ventilation. Yet, almost all churches install them. Some have made use of false windows with a light installed behind them for effect. Many churches still desire stained-glass windows with Biblical symbols, although the large, figured panels of former years are on the decline. A preference seems to be developing for glass that gives a soft light and blends well with the surroundings. Good use of light and color does much to encourage a worshipful mood. This, too, is a specialized field, and the committee, with the architect, should obtain and use the best professional help available.

ACOUSTICS

"What we see is an aid to worship, what we hear is worship." [4] Great care in planning for good acoustics should be taken from the very first. The shape of the building and the materials chosen have much to do with it. The safe thing is to involve an acoustical engineer in the early planning. Recent advances in sound engineering make it possible to control troublesome frequencies in such a manner as to make the natural voice of the speaker warm and responsive yet loud and clear. Of course, the result is more effective services and a more responsive congregation. "Dead" churches usually are caused by too much soft material being used that absorb the sound waves. A room may seem "alive" when empty, but "dead" when filled with people, because of human bodies and clothing. To correct dead acoustics, softer materials may be changed to those with harder surfaces. In some places, paint may help. Speakers should be installed in accordance with the recommendation of experts.

Noises that interfere with worship should be controlled or prevented. Traffic noises from the street can be troublesome but their effect can be controlled by all-year air conditioning that requires a tight building. Unwelcome noises from other rooms in the building may be avoided by separating assembly rooms from the nave by corridors or by other rooms. Noise in the vestibule or narthex, occasioned by late arrivals, may be reduced by the installation of an abundance of absorbent materials on ceiling, walls, and floor.

[4] Enos E. Shupp, Jr., *Your Church,* "Let us Consider Acoustics" October, November, December, 1960, p. 44. The Religious Publishing Co. Jenkintown, Pa.

ELECTRONICS

Proper lighting has always been a major concern in building churches, but never before have there been so many electrical devices for enhancing worship. The intensity and the control of light have much to do with moods. Lighting in the worship center should be soft. Concealed or recessed lighting eliminates the glare that could not be avoided with exposed lights.

Accent lights should be placed over the platform area or chancel. Light directed on the pulpit or reading stand should come from more than one direction to avoid shadows.

Rheostatic control of all lighting is common practice and is quite desirable. The dimming of lights during certain parts of a service, such as observance of the ordinances, may help worshippers to center their attention on the focal point. Such procedures should not be mistaken for theatrical techniques where all is darkness except the stage in order that the viewer may lose sight of everything but the action before him. In corporate worship, all persons should be conscious that others also are participating in the service. In the nave, sufficient light for reading of hymns and scripture is needed throughout. It is well to remember, too, that most older people need 50 to 60 percent more light than a person twenty years of age.

The sound amplifier is another apparatus of great usefulness, and even the smaller churches now have them. One wonders how Jesus, Paul, and other preachers, like Moody and Sunday, were able to be heard by so many thousands. Many men with strong minds have light voices, but in our day they, too, can be heard. The amplifier is useful to other speakers, as well as the preacher. Often persons unaccustomed to public speaking cannot be heard even in a small building. This wonderful little box makes it possible for all to hear and to be heard. It has done much to eliminate the need for shouting and thus has made listening easier. An added advantage is that, with a microphone and a speaker and a bit of wiring, a large room in another part of the building can easily be made into an auxiliary auditorium. The machine should be placed at some point where ushers or others trained in its operation can control it. Earphones attached to certain pews are still used by many people with hearing deficiencies.

Tape recorders, too, are very useful. Thousands of shut-ins have appreciated hearing a service of their church, brought to them by means of a recording. Worship services recorded and broadcast by radio and by television are heard by millions of people every week.

These are either aids to worship or aids to the ministry of the church. They can be much more effective if planned for in advance of construction. Ask your architect to instruct the electrical engineer to provide for this equipment. If these items are included in the electrical plans, and installed with other equipment, the cost of them will be fractional.

Chapter 6

PLANNING FOR
CHRISTIAN EDUCATION

THE CHURCH BEGAN as an educational fellowship in which Christians "continued steadfastly in the apostles' teaching" (Acts 2:42). The Church was, and should continue to be, truly the school of Christ. A "disciple" was a "learner," as should be the case today. Each member of the fellowship of believers gradually appropriated the ideals and attitudes of the group; everything the Church did was educational.

Today, however, almost every church needs a more formal program of education. Some of the objectives of present-day Christian education can not be fully met through an informal approach. A church's responsibility for an effective program of education includes provision of adequate physical facilities designed especially to help accomplish predetermined purposes and objectives.[1]

OBJECTIVES OF CHRISTIAN EDUCATION

Understanding the Christian faith is one basic objective of an education program. One does not have to know all

[1] For a discussion in greater detail see *Building and Equipping for Christian Education* by C. Harry Atkinson, published by the National Council of Churches, New York.

79

about the Bible to be a Christian, yet to grow in grace requires an understanding of facts and their meanings for Christians. The Hebrew and Christian traditions have influenced the course of the world far more than those of any other religion. Yet, very little is known and understood about them by church people and others. A recent decision of the United States Supreme Court practically eliminates Bible reading from the public schools, putting the responsibility for teaching Christianity squarely on the church and the home. An effective program of Christian teaching requires physical facilities that are appropriate for the undertaking.

Christian growth is another important objective of education. Christians are admonished to "grow in grace and in the knowledge of our Lord and Saviour Jesus Christ" (II Peter 3:18). This kind of growth requires not only factual information but also meaningful association and involvement with others. Service that meets the needs of others is one of the principal means of growth. Some churches have developed elaborate programs to try to meet this need. Such programs require suitable meeting places for strengthening these efforts.

Christian evangelism is a third major objective of education. The early years of the Sunday School movement were definitely evangelistic. A Sunday School properly related to the church can be an important agency for furthering many of the objectives of the congregation. Too many churches view the Sunday School primarily as a means of educating children of the church families. They miss a great opportunity when they do not have all-age schools that include all the members and that also seek to bring in nonmembers. The Sunday School can be an effective outreaching and evangelizing agency of the church. People must be reached before they can be taught, and they must be taught before they can understand how to become Christians.

People cannot be reached unless there is a place for them. The shade of a tree or the end of a log may be an interesting place for teaching once in a while but not for a sustained program of education. The type of building is extremely important in reaching people. An already-filled building discourages growth. To reach new people, space must be provided. Good, well-planned buildings are not an expense but an investment. They are not an end in themselves but a means of helping the church accomplish its purposes.

ORGANIZATIONAL PROGRAMS AND ACTIVITIES

Churches have developed many programs designed to help accomplish their educational objectives. Such programs include study of the Bible and related materials, worship, recreation, creative arts, group projects, and service opportunities. These various activities are really program elements of a variety of organizations that are intended to contribute to the spiritual growth of those participating. If they are not needed, churches should eliminate them. If they *are* needed, churches should make them more effective by providing adequate buildings and equipment for their use.

When planning for enlargement of physical facilities it is advisable to study and evaluate present practices. Why perpetuate ineffective programs by surrounding them with brick and concrete? A church almost invariably gets the kind of program it builds for.

TRENDS

Present facilities should be carefully studied to determine how they can be used more effectively or adapted to meet changing objectives. Of special concern should be a comprehensive review of present trends in Christian education. The following trends may affect needs for physical facilities.

1. Recent trends definitely are toward informality, flexibility, and group activities. Pupil involvement requires space and equipment that permits more freedom. This is especially true of children's departments.

2. Some denominations are changing their grouping arrangements. Coeducational groups are becoming more common. Larger classes with one teacher and a few assistants have been adopted by some. Separate classrooms for small groups are giving way to larger ones. Not all churches are moving in this direction, however. Many churches still insist that more people can be enlisted and better work done with the sexes separated and in smaller groups.

3. There is an increasing recognition of the importance of the environment and how it conditions the attitudes and responses of persons. A view of the beauties of nature outside calls for low windows, especially in the children's department. Experts who work with children feel strongly that good use of light and the right choice of colors help create an environment conducive to learning.

4. Special interest groups, such as "Golden Age" clubs, are becoming an important part of the education program of many churches. Careful consideration should be given to providing physical facilities designed to meet actual needs of persons at each stage of their growth.

5. Many churches have established multiple Sunday School sessions as well as dual worship services. Imaginative leadership and a willingness to experiment have resulted in many such ventures. The easiest and cheapest way to double the size of a building is to use it twice.

6. Weekday religious education is developing in many ways,

as evidenced by the church kindergarten, parochial schools, and released time from public schools. A few heroic churches in the inner city, instead of moving to the suburbs, are developing programs of weekday activities to minister and bring growth to at least some of their constituents.

7. The most astonishing trend confronting churches is the rapid increase in population. By 1980 it is estimated that we will have 250 million people in the United States. Churches are challenged to reach and teach the oncoming multitudes.

Many new churches will be needed to meet this challenge, and every existing church should make an earnest effort to enlarge and revitalize its ministries. Larger and better facilities will be needed for every phase of the education program.

NURSERY

Every church should provide a place in its education program for the youngest children. Nothing is more important, for two reasons. First, something constructive can be done for the child if it can be given love and concern and many happy experiences. Second, something constructive can also be done for the parents. If no place were provided for children, one of the parents, and probably both parents, would stay at home with the child. Eventually, another one arrives, and in a few years most or all religious interest may be lost. The pastor of a large Sunday School gladly reported that more than one hundred children were in the nursery department on a given Sunday. And he remarked, "For every child in the nursery, one or two young adults were in Bible study groups and in the worship service."

Planning well for small children pays rich dividends. Where there are many nursery children, separate rooms should be provided for different ages. So rapidly do children develop that some churches provide for closer grading—a department for each one-half year. Nursery departments should never be in the basement. Not more than twenty children should be in each room. Minimum floor space should be from 20 to 30 square feet per child.

A highly satisfactory arrangement is that of a nursery suite. A reception area serves as the entrance where children are received from the parents and guided to their rooms. Kitchenette and child-sized toilet facilities are provided. Low windows that permit viewing the outside are included. Soundproofed walls and toilets installed between rooms combine to diminish noise appreciably. Storage cabinets for toys and other materials, and suitable hangers for wraps, are a part of the building. Floors are of materials that are easily cleaned, such as rubber tile, cork tile, asphalt tile, or finished hardwood.

KINDERGARTEN

The kindergarten is attended by children four and five years of age. Separate rooms should be provided for each of the two ages, if at all possible. Room for activity is required. Not more than twenty-five children should be in any one room. A minimum of 25 square feet per child should be provided. Newer approaches to learning require 30 to 35 square feet.

Kindergarten rooms should never be in a basement. As for the nursery, low windows (not more than 24 inches high) are desirable and floors should be of easily cleaned materials. Picture rail and tack boards should be a part of the building. Cheerful and attractive colors should be chosen.

PRIMARY

The primary department is comprised of children six, seven, and eight years of age. Generally they are in the first, second, and third grades of public schools. This department should be on the first floor, off a main corridor, with at least one door in the back of each room. Plenty of light and a good view of the outdoors are very desirable.

To prevent overstimulation and provide for group activities, space should be ample. Twenty-five to 30 square feet per person is considered good. Twenty to 25 is rated fair. Less than 20 square feet is unsatisfactory. Formal worship centers limit flexibility and are not recommended. Informal worship centers may be arranged along an unbroken wall. Not more than thirty pupils should be assigned to any one room.

JUNIORS

Not all denominations use the same approach in working with juniors. In many churches the junior department includes children of ages nine through eleven. This corresponds closely to grades four through six in the public schools and is considered by many to be the best basis for grouping. According to Miss Margie McCarty of the General Board of Education, The Methodist Church, "Junior boys and girls learn best when working together in sizable groups. They learn from each other and they learn to adjust to each other if properly guided and related to meaningful projects. A lead teacher with assisting teachers for each eight to ten children working as a team can successfully direct the classroom activities of twenty-five pupils." [2]

[2] Margie McCarty, "The Church and Our Elementary School Children," *Protestant Church Administration and Equipment.* Edited by C. H. Atkinson. December, 1957, p. 19.

This approach requires a large room with at east 25 square feet of floor space for each person. The room may be on any floor. Portable storage facilities should be provided for each organization that might be assigned the use of the room.

Another approach to junior work in a large number of churches includes children of ages nine through twelve. This arrangement calls for an assembly room large enough to accommodate the whole department. Small classrooms opening off the assembly room are provided for classes of not more than ten boys or girls each. Minimum space of 8 square feet is needed for each person in the assembly area and 10 square feet for each person in the classroom. Blackboards and tack boards are needed. The department may be located on any floor, but preferably not in a basement. Many large Sunday Schools have a department for each age, nine through twelve.

YOUTH

Although the approach to youth work is not the same in all churches, the facilities needed are very similar. Many churches have departments called Junior High, ages twelve through fourteen, and Senior High, ages fifteen through seventeen, which corresponds closely to grading in public schools. Suggested arrangements include an assembly room with adjacent classrooms. Junior High classes with fifteen pupils are large enough. Senior High classes should have not more than twenty. The trend is for greater participation through the use of role playing, handcrafts, and group projects. For this type of activity 18 square feet per pupil is recommended. Space for the youth division may be on any floor and, of course, should have appointments that are inviting and appealing to young people. In planning these departments, flexibility must be kept in mind as several groups, no doubt, will make use of this space.

ADULTS

Although adults offer the greatest opportunity and the greatest need for Christian education, many churches give little or no attention to adult education. The increase in adult involvement in secular education has been phenomenal. Adults want to learn, and they can learn. Adults need to know the faith in order to share insight and understanding with children and youth. They also need the strength that comes from Christian fellowship available in small study groups.

Adults bring the children. Adults become leaders. Adults give financial support. Because of their great concern for children and youth, churches can easily neglect the adults. Any congregation realistically trying to meet the needs of our time must emphasize education for the grown-ups. The education program will not reach adults unless suitable space is provided for them.

Because of the wide range of ages and the large numerical potential, a church of almost any size may need more than one adult department. Larger churches certainly need several adult groups. Newer approaches to learning, such as role playing, panels, buzz groups, work projects, and group discussion, suggest a minimum floor space of 18 to 20 square feet per person. No class should plan for more than twenty-five in attendance. Space for adult education should be flexible so that it may be usable and available for many kinds of church meetings.

Chapter 7

PLANNING FOR
FELLOWSHIP
AND RECREATION

WHEN CHRISTIANS TALK about fellowship they mean much more than just having fun or a good time. In the early Christian era, *koinonia,* the word used for fellowship, signified a closeness that bound Christians together in love for one another. Jesus, greatly concerned about this quality of life, told his followers that their love for one another would identify them as his disciples. As Christians pray together, worship together, sing together, serve together, confess their faults one to another, share their joys and their fears, and bear one another's burdens, this fellowship is deepened and strengthened.

All that has been said in the preceding chapters about planning for worship, education, and service applies likewise to strengthening the functions that build Christian fellowship. Through worshipping and working together, the church opens its life to all and provides a favorable climate for growth. Informal associations with others offer great opportunity for development of personality and enrichment of life. Play, as well as worship and work, can be helpful in strengthening fellowship. Many churches now are seeking to help people grow through programs of

Christian recreation. This is a relatively new emphasis, but its importance should be a challenge to the committee assigned to plan needed facilities.

REASONS FOR RECREATION

First, the committee should ask why a program for fellowship and recreation is needed. The most obvious reason is that man is a social being. In order really to be himself he must have relationships with other human beings. He can't be human alone. His growth into Christian maturity and usefulness depends on social interaction. The church should make possible associations that will encourage such growth.

Modern culture presents a need that was practically unknown a few years ago—a need for worthy use of leisure time. This is a serious and growing problem for rich and poor, young and old. Idleness contributes to degradation. Idleness sometimes is called the devil's workshop. Worthy use of leisure time is vitally related to personality development and spiritual growth.

Because of the mobility of the population, millions of families are transplanted every year. As a result, there are more lonely people than ever before. The informal group experiences provided in a program of recreation and fellowship is increasingly important for meeting the needs of uprooted and unstable people.

A program intended just to "keep the kids off the street" is not a worthy one. The kids will "catch on" and sooner or later will realize that this is just another gimmick. However, a program of recreation that provides wholesome and creative social relationships is a means of growth and should be considered a definite part of the education program of the church. Its purposes are the same as the purposes of the church—to "make disciples and teach them to observe all things" as Christ commanded. This means Christian understanding and service. Churches need some convictions about the value of Christian recreation to plan well for the kind of program needed.

MEET THE NEEDS

The survey report should provide a source of information for developing plans to meet real needs. The number of children and youth in the church and community should be a matter of record. The children will be in the youth groups tomorrow. If older people predominate, a different approach may be taken. The point is that the church should plan to meet particular needs rather than try to keep up with the neighboring churches or to fit somebody's preconceived notion as to what should be done.

The committee should study the resources of the community. Not every church needs a gymnasium. They are expensive to build and to maintain. Often gyms built and maintained by other institutions in the community are available for church use. The same is true for other types of activity such as swimming, bowling, and volleyball. These possibilities should be considered before investing heavily in equipment that may get little use.

USE WHAT YOU HAVE

The church should plan to use what it has built or will build for other functions. Many recreation activities such as banquets, luncheons, receptions, parties, arts and crafts, and some drama and athletics, can be accommodated in space planned for other uses. The committee should strive for flexibility. Class parties and group games may be held in almost any room that has movable chairs and a piano. Floors in a large room or hall may be designed to permit

shuffleboard and possibly other activity games. Some types
of drama are suitable for department rooms or even for
the worship center.

Outdoor areas offer many opportunities. Croquet, horse-
shoes, archery, badminton, and even volleyball, may be
played on the lawn. Paved parking areas may be used for
basketball, tennis, volleyball, skating, and other games. If
planned and improved with recreation in mind, the
grounds can be used well at a minimum of expense. To
provide for some of these activities may require outdoor
lights and a good smooth pavement, the expense of which
would be minor as compared to the cost of a gymnasium
or a specialized recreation building.

PARISH HALL

Almost every church needs a room designed primarily
for socials, banquets, receptions, and recreation purposes.
Such a room can be used in many ways in the education
program if planned well. The social room should not be in
the basement, especially if this would normally put it
under the worship center. The desirable height for a fairly
large social room would increase the required number of
steps to the place of worship. Support of the superstructure would probably require large pillars that are unwelcome obstructions. The size of the room would almost certainly be dictated by the size of the worship center. A
large airy room, preferably on the first floor, is more desirable.

The dimensions of the social room, should, of course, be
determined by the size and needs of the congregation. For
meetings, 7 or 8 square feet per person are needed when
chairs are placed in rows. Seated at tables, people need 10
square feet or more for comfortable spacing. The ceiling
should be higher than that of a normal room, probably 10

feet or more. Very large rooms with a stage equipped for drama require greater height. Floors should be of durable tile, and may have built-in designs for floor games such as shuffleboard. Ceilings should be of absorbent materials to help control noises. They should be of a type not easily marred or damaged when the social room is used for games that require the use of a ball. Lights should be recessed for protection and for giving an impression of greater ceiling height.

STAGE

A stage at one end of the social room has a number of uses. It may serve as a speaker's platform for large gatherings or for leaders in a social or fellowship program. If well planned and proportioned, it makes possible drama productions used by some churches in religious education. Since a stage adequate for drama productions has sizable requirements, a church considering such an installation should make thorough inquiry as to expense and should receive some assurance that such a stage would be used. The dimensions must be governed by size of the social room. Just a few of the requirements are mentioned here. The stage height should not be less than 30 to 36 inches. Three feet above this is required for hanging curtains, lights, and scenery. The proscenium should be a minimum of 9 feet in height. The stage depth should be 20 feet. As can be seen, to provide adequately for drama requires considerable space and careful planning.[1] Not every church will want to do it.

[1] For details on stage planning see *Building and Equipping for Christian Education* by C. Harry Atkinson, published by The National Council of Churches, New York.

WIRING

The social room is a multipurpose room. Special attention must be given to electric service to make it useful. Ceiling lights should be recessed. Adequate circuits are needed to provide flexibility in lighting arrangements. A central control is needed. Care must be taken to see that power is adequate for stage lighting if a stage for drama is planned. Numerous electric outlets are required for a stage production. Spotlights, footlights, lamp outlets, and microphones are a few examples of needs for outlets. Electric outlets should be carefully placed throughout the room to provide for the many kinds of meetings that will be held. Wiring for microphones and various kinds of audiovisuals, if installed at the beginning, as a part of the electrical contract, should cost less than if added later.

GENERAL STORAGE

Considerable storage space is needed in this area. Folding tables and chairs for the banquet room must be stored. Stage equipment, games and recreation materials, visual-aid projectors and screens, and numerous other items have to be put away in an orderly manner and in a convenient place. Cleaning materials and equipment should also be kept handy. To provide adequately for storage space, in advance, certainly would seem to be an act of prudence.

THE KITCHEN

In planning a church kitchen, the committee should consult some of the faithful women who serve in it, as well as a kitchen engineer. This will not guarantee a perfect kitchen, but it will obviate some unhappiness later, when weaknesses become evident. The kitchen should be at one end of the social room. If it is a large room, a location on the side near the center would be nearer to more people— but the noise problem would be intensified. Workers usually are in the kitchen while a meeting is in progress. If the kitchen could be separated from the social room by a wall, noises could be reduced considerably.

Churches should build kitchens for their own use and not for commercial purposes as a money-making scheme. The size of the kitchen should be determined by the size of the membership and the size of the social room. Some authorities recommend 20 to 25 percent of the floor area of the social hall. This proportion would seem large to others, especially if auxiliary rooms could be used to pre- pare salads and serve plates. But where volunteer help is used, more room is required. One author makes a good point when he says, "While kitchen engineers are well versed in the requirements of hotels and similar institu- tions where food is handled by professionals, they should be advised that a church kitchen operated by volunteer help must have more floor space than the compact facili- ties used by professional kitchen help." [2] Faithful women workers may be happier with two or more domestic ranges rather than commercial ones with which they are unfa- miliar. If possible, the equipment to be used should be de- cided upon before space is allotted for the kitchen.

The size of the kitchen may also be influenced by the kind of meals to be served. Many churches have family meals where much of the food is brought from home. Banquets that attract large crowds and that require all food to be prepared on the premises are infrequent in most churches. Every city of any size has caterers that prepare and deliver, ready to eat, all kinds of food at

[2] C. Harry Atkinson, *How to Get Your Church Built* (Garden City, N.Y.: Doubleday & Company, Inc., 1964), p. 107.

reasonable prices. If food for the limited number of large meals could be prepared elsewhere, it would reduce the amount of space and equipment needed for the church kitchen. The committee might want to consider and recommend such a policy, and plan a kitchen that will care for normal-size gatherings.

KITCHEN STORAGE

Kitchen storage must be ample and well organized. The cabinets and space provided for cooking utensils, dishes, cutlery, and linens should be as near as possible to the place of use. Cabinets above and below the work areas should be planned as a part of the building, thus avoiding the makeshift appearance that is sometimes evident when things are added. Food storage could well be in a separate room, and it may need to be under lock and key. Ample space must be provided for coolers and freezers. All of this adds up to a good bit of space that must be well planned if disappointment and hardship are to be avoided.

KITCHEN OPENINGS

Of course, if food is to be served from the kitchen, as in a cafeteria line, the windows must be located for convenience to the steam table and the dining area. If dishes are to be returned by the users, as in many churches and schools, a separate window should be provided for that use. An outside door is needed for receiving deliveries and for removing garbage. Two doors, one for entrance and the other for exit, are needed to avoid collisions of workers.

SANITATION

Tile used for flooring should be very durable, and a drain to facilitate scrubbing should be properly located. Electric outlets must be placed in the walls near the place where the dishwasher and other appliances will be installed. All finishes should be washable. Unless the hall is air-conditioned, windows should be screened. Every effort should be made to supply the most sanitary conditions. Some states require churches and commercial restaurants to meet the same health standards. Planning the right kind of church kitchen is no easy job.

KITCHENETTES

One or more kitchenettes is desirable and, in large churches, almost essential. In churches with an active program, several groups may frequently meet at the same time. A men's banquet may be held in the social hall at the same time a smaller meeting or a wedding reception is in progress in another part of the building. The church parlor and the nursery each will almost certainly need at least a compact stove and refrigerator unit. A kitchenette near one of the larger assembly rooms would be used many times for preparation of refreshments.

PARLOR

A comfortably equipped and well-located church parlor sees much use. In addition to ladies' meetings, committee meetings, small receptions, and personal conferences, the parlor may be helpful in other ways. One pastor invites guests to come to the church parlor for light refreshments and fellowship after services. Another church has a passage from the library to the church parlor, and many members use the parlor for reading. This room should have a durable type of high-quality furniture to stand the wear. Good carpet on the floor will increase its beauty and warmth, muffle sounds, and make cleaning easier and quicker. Some churches call it the "ladies' parlor" and restrict its use to the fairer sex. This practice may need to be reexamined if the parlor is to be the "church parlor."

AN EXPANDED PROGRAM OF RECREATION

What has been suggested about facilities for recreation is applicable to more normal situations. Some of the very large churches, however, conduct an expanded program of recreation. A few churches have a professional director or minister of recreation. This kind of program requires much more elaborate facilities—in some cases a recreation building or wing with a large play area and several smaller rooms for arts, crafts, hobbies, ceramics, and other activities. If full body activities are desired, a gymnasium with showers and dressing rooms, kitchen and snack area, and possibly a lounge may be included. So comprehensive an arrangement requires a full-time director to supervise the program. This type of program belongs only to the large church, but it is becoming increasingly prevalent.[3]

[3] Pamphlet providing detailed information may be obtained from Bob Boyd, Secretary, Church Recreation Service, 127 Ninth Avenue, N., Nashville, Tenn.

Chapter 8

PLANNING FOR
ADMINISTRATION
AND OTHER FUNCTIONS

ADMINISTRATION IS an important part of the life of modern churches. Facilities that provide for efficient operation of the church functions should be planned when other facilities are planned. Proper planning for this function may require a special committee. If so, the church probably has interested members who are trained and experienced in various phases of administration and who should be on this committee, provided they are vitally involved in the program of the church.

Administration processes are necessary if all the other ministries are to operate effectively. Planning conferences must be held. Activities must be publicized and promoted. Records must be kept and used. Materials and supplies need to be ordered and properly distributed. Mailing has to be done. For good communication, many items must be duplicated. The pastor must study. Members request counseling. Secretaries and assistants need comfortable and convenient quarters in which to do effective work. The administrative area is used more than any other part of the building. Better work can be done when facilities are adequate, and this requires careful planning.

THE CHURCH OFFICE

Although a comparatively small percentage of the churches have several staff members, almost every church should have at least a general office, a study, and storage space. The office should be on a level with the worship center and easily accessible from the various departments of the church. The office should be clearly marked and, if not convenient to the main street and the parking areas, signs indicating the direction to the office should be in evidence.

The space needed will depend on the volume of work and the size of the staff, but the tendency is to allow too small an area to meet the needs. If more than one secretary is employed, separate offices may be desirable, but good work can be done with several working in the same office if there is sufficient space. Movable desk separators may be of value in preventing interruption. Space for file cabinets is required. A counter or some kind of separator is needed to keep visitors and loafers out of the work area.

If at all possible, a workroom adjoining the office should be provided for duplicators and other office machines. Careful spacing, tables or a counter of the proper height, and provision for storage of supplies should be included. A lavatory or a sink in the workroom would be welcomed by those who use it.

A SUITE OF OFFICES

Where there are two or more staff members, a suite of offices may be arranged. The most accessible area may be used as a reception room. One secretary should serve as receptionist. Other offices may be either adjoining or adjacent to this space, arranged in such a way that callers may see the receptionist first. The time to plan a communication system for staff use is at the beginning. Necessary wiring and equipment may well be included in the electrical contract.

Toilet facilities planned for convenience of the workers save time and are appreciated. Coffee breaks are common practice in most offices, therefore a kitchenette where drinks are readily available can make it easy and convenient to have brief informal staff conferences. Since offices are in use every day and other parts of the building are not, a separate system for heating and cooling would be economical.

OFFICES FOR ASSISTANTS

Offices for the associate pastor, the minister of education, the minister of music, the minister of administration, and other staff members may also be in the suite. Although a church may not have several full-time workers, provision for some expansion room may be wise, and the space might be put to other uses until such time as the growth of the church warrants an enlargement of the staff. Larger churches that employ a bookkeeper, even part time, should provide a finance office where he can work and where records can be kept. The counting committee could use this space for counting the offerings and for preparing bank deposits. A conference room near the office is an important convenience for committee meetings and planning sessions. If comfortably furnished, this room may be used as a lounge. Office workers are on duty many hours each week, and at times would welcome such a place for a bit of rest. Also, wherever people gather, there is always a danger that someone will become ill and need a place to recline.

PASTOR'S OFFICE

The modern pastor has numerous administrative responsibilities. Surveys of a large number of ministers indicate that pastors spend 40 percent or more of their time in administration and promotion. The pastor has been called the "pastoral director" by an eminent scholar. But his work at the church is much more than administration. He must study and prepare sermons. He must spend time counseling with troubled members. He needs a good place to work. Fearing criticism, many pastors do not request all the space and equipment they ought to have. The committee should study carefully his needs and should recommend that every desirable feature be included in the plans.

There is no more important place in the church than the pastor's study. And it should be in the church. A study at home is also desirable, so that the pastor may make use of bits of time at irregular hours (see Chapter 12). However, it is a good discipline as well as a good example for the pastor to go to work and spend regular hours at his desk and his task.

The pastor's study is usually next to the general office. The entrance should be through the office where the secretary or receptionist is located. However, there should be another door for use as an exit. The pastor's office should be in a choice location of the suite and should be somewhat larger than offices of other staff members. Since the pastor spends a lot of time there, it should be well finished and comfortably furnished. Built-in bookshelves with sliding panel doors are preferred by some pastors. A clothes closet, as well as toilet facilities and a shower, would be welcomed.

In many churches, because of administrative duties and much counseling, pastors have difficulty reserving time for study. A small room upstairs in the back of the building may be appropriated for a workshop. In such a room, privacy may be maintained for at least a few hours each week. Work can be laid out and left on the desk without embarrassment. Hours for counseling and committee work may be designated in the downstairs office. Of course, in case of emergency, the secretary would have instructions to call him.

OFFICE FURNISHINGS

Since the office suite is an area where several people spend many hours and many others make frequent visits, it should be properly finished. Floors should be of attractive material such as asphalt tile, cork tile, linoleum, hardwood, or carpeting. A few minutes with a vacuum cleaner usually is all that is required to restore its good appearance. Walls may be of plaster or paneling. The latter is easier to keep looking nice. The former gives opportunity to use pastel colors. Possibly some use of both would be appropriate. Ceilings should be of acoustical materials to reduce sound vibrations. Carpet on the floors further reduces the effects of noises.

FACILITIES FOR MAINTENANCE STAFF

Maintenance workers are often inadequately provided with various necessities and conveniences. If there is a building superintendent, he should have at least a desk space in a convenient location with which the communication system should be connected. Room for a shop where minor repairs can be made is helpful. Lockers, toilet facilities, and a shower, should be provided for maintenance employees. For efficient operation of a large building, ample storage space for tools and supplies is a must. Some of this can be in the shop. Many steps and a great deal of time, however, will be saved by having storage places in several parts of the building. A janitor's closet and slop sink on each floor or in each wing will facilitate scrubbing and save much time and energy.

PARKING AREA

Careful arrangements must be made for parking (see Chapter 3). Many people are influenced in their choice of a church by the provision made for this service. The location of the building units on the site will largely determine the space available for parking. More than one parking area, conveniently located around the plant, is desirable. If at all possible, parking space should be designed for entrance and exit, paved, and properly lined in readiness for the opening of the new building. To have a beautiful and commodious structure and a dusty or muddy parking area is inconsistent, to say the least. The cost of adequate parking facilities is a part of the cost of the total project and should be well planned and provided.

LANDSCAPING

The background and setting of a building enhances its beauty like the setting of a gem. Many church buildings that are really not unusual are made inspiringly beautiful by proper landscaping. The right choice and location of shrubs and the care and planting of trees can be used to "frame" the building and make a beautiful sight. Trees on the site must be protected from damage by the builders. Walks must be properly located. This is not a job for the men's club or the missionary society unless some one in the group has understanding and skill in this field. A landscape engineer might well be used, just as other experts are used in developing building plans. If this is the decision of the committee, his advice should be sought early enough for him to have a part in the over-all planning of the project.

BULLETIN BOARD

An attractive bulletin board can be a wayside pulpit. Its chief value is for those who are not members of the church. Hence, it should be located in a conspicuous place close enough to the street to be seen by those who pass by. Most bulletin boards are too small and are the wrong shape. Unless they are large enough for more than the pastor's name and the time of the worship service, they are not of much value. It is not very exciting to see on the bulletin board "Services as usual." But there is room on the face of it for little more.

To be useful, bulletin boards must be read. To be read in this day of fast traffic, they should be large and should have more horizontal than vertical space. They should be well lighted, preferably with neon lights, and should have large luminous letters. A bulletin board, well located, well made, and well used speaks its message constantly. Plan it carefully to fit the location and to harmonize with the building.

LIBRARY

In many churches the library has become a vigorous part of the religious education program. Some churches have several thousand volumes and report a circulation of several hundred volumes each month. The best location for this book ministry is on the main floor, where the heaviest traffic occurs. A well-lighted room with ample space and plenty of glass in the walls for display purposes will stimulate interest in reading. Where there is no full-time librarian, the library may be located adjacent to offices where it can be used during the week. If good reference books are available, teachers will use them. A workroom inside the library, equipped with cabinets for supplies and a counter for repair work, is very helpful. A kitchen-type sink set in the counter, flush with the top, also enhances its usefulness. If the church has a full-time minister of recreation who directs all leisure-time activities, he may prefer that the library be under his supervision. If so, the library room may be planned as a part of the recreation area where he can provide supervision.

CHAPEL

A chapel in a church building is optional. Small churches with a worship center of reasonable proportion probably do not need one. Churches with a large membership and an oversized nave will find many uses for a small, worshipful chapel. In planning such a room, the purposes for which it will be used must be considered.

FOR WEDDINGS

A chapel is very appropriate for small weddings. It is easy to decorate. It is not expensive to clean, heat, and cool. For a small group, it provides a warmer and more favorable atmosphere than would be possible in a very large room. A chapel can be kept in readiness for private weddings that may be arranged on short notice. If possible, a small social room with kitchenette should be in close proximity for receptions. The chapel can be used for many other functions of the church, of course.

FOR FUNERALS

Many people feel that funerals for Christians should be held at the church. For various reasons, most funerals are held with a limited number of friends and relatives in attendance. Seldom does a church funeral fill a large nave. A chapel is a most suitable place for such a service, if doors and aisles are wide enough to accommodate a casket. A vestibule for registration of friends and possibly for the viewing of the remains (if such is planned) may be desirable. A comfortably furnished room nearby for the use of a bereaved family would be welcomed. This room may have many other uses.

USE FOR EDUCATION

A chapel room seating from 50 to 150 persons can be very useful in the education program. It makes an ideal assembly room for youth or adults. Youths will use it repeatedly as a worship center. If adequate in size, it may be the meeting place for Vacation Bible School assemblies. Women's meetings, teachers' meetings, midweek worship services, and many other conferences will find such a room an ideal place to gather. If used for a department of the Sunday School, classrooms in close proximity should be planned. Equipped with suitable electric outlets and wiring, this space would enhance the use of visual aids in the program of education.

AUXILIARY AUDITORIUM

On rare occasions, churches need a place for overflow crowds. When properly wired, sound equipment can be easily installed in the chapel to serve this need.

PERSONAL DEVOTIONS

If the chapel is in an accessible place and has a worshipful atmosphere, its use for private devotions should be encouraged. When planned with a street entrance, a sign inviting passersby to enter for prayer will bring good results. Such an open-door policy should be adopted by more Protestant churches.

TEMPORARY WORSHIP CENTER

A large number of churches unable to build the permanent worship center at first have used a chapel temporarily. Multiple services may be necessary to care for the congregation. Movable partitions between the chapel and large adjoining rooms afford a means of increasing the size of the temporary worship center. When it is no longer needed for the main worship services, permanent partitions may be installed and the area made into a permanent chapel.

APPEARANCE

The chapel need not be a miniature copy of the worship center. A different appearance and arrangement may present a wholesome contrast. Whether to have pews or seats is a matter of choice and may be determined by the principal use for which the chapel is designed. Pews seem to have the same advantages in the chapel that they have in the permanent worship center.

WORKING WITH
THE ARCHITECT

THE PLANNING and erecting of a building that involves the work of dozens of highly skilled tradesmen cannot be trusted to a part-time draftsman and the local barn-builders. This work is highly specialized, requiring a professional who must know the intricacies of many trades and who must know the merits and demerits of many materials well enough to put them all together in such a way as to produce a good and useful structure.

WHY AN ARCHITECT IS NECESSARY

The building of a good church house is a unique challenge. To provide well for the many functions of a church requires dedicated imagination more than for any other type of structure. Church leaders should realize that adequate facilities demand the best in planning and construction.

Building for public meetings must meet rigid code requirements designed to insure the safety of citizens. Some states and municipalities refuse to issue a permit for a building not designed by a registered architect. A country church built an education unit and installed rest room facilities for the first time. Imagine the disappointment of that church when use of the building was delayed because the installation was inferior to state code requirements. Remodeling and improvement was required even before the new building could be entered. The extra expense was substantial.

A good architect usually saves money for the owner— the church. Good planning avoids wasted space and costly mistakes. Adequate but less expensive materials may be selected. A poorly arranged building may be a source of discouragement and frustration to the congregation, causing loss of interest and support, whereas a well-planned and well-built structure will encourage members to be a happy and a willing people. The architect's fee, in most cases, is one of the best investments a church can make.

No one short of a skilled professional would have the know-how to put ideas into form, and bring together the skills of many specialists and the materials of a scientific age to achieve a beautiful and functional building. For a church to undertake such a project without the help of an architect would invite disaster.

HOW TO SELECT AN ARCHITECT

The church should first choose a committee to select and recommend an architect. This may be a special committee chosen or appointed for this specific purpose. The plans subcommittee may be given this responsibility, or the building committee as a whole may make the selection. Especially in churches with congregational polity the recommendation should be made to the congregation for approval or rejection. For the architect to be truly the representative of the people he must be their choice.

Before the committee considers any prospect, it should establish some criteria and a procedure. A basic question is, "What kind of person do we need to guide us in the architectural phases of this undertaking?"

CRITERIA TO BE CONSIDERED

1. *Technical Training.* The architect should be a graduate of a recognized school of architecture. The reputation of the school he attended says something of the requirements he had to meet. Most reputable architects hold membership in the American Institute of Architects. This organization has high standards and makes strict, ethical demands on its members.

2. *Experience.* What the architect has achieved should be of great interest to the committee. Members of the committee should, if possible, view some of the products of his art. To confer with clients would be most effective in gaining information about the prospect's work and how congregations respond to him. An experienced man should produce photographs, not drawings.

3. *Personality.* Ability to teach and a willingness to learn are both desirable. The architect must be able to communicate. His job requires close association with individual leaders, committees, and, at times, with the whole congregation. Matters that are the simplest routine to him may seem strange and complex to others. He must be able to teach others and to have the patience to wait for understanding to take place. Technically competent people often are unable to communicate well. An architect who can guide the committee and the congregation in making the right decisions is much to be desired.

The architect who knows it all is a difficult person with whom to work. He is truly a specialist, but usually not in religion. He may learn from committee members who are more familiar with church problems. He may also learn from faithful members who are very concerned, although not on the committee. Although quite competent in technical matters of his profession, he may not be fully informed about worship, liturgy, and other procedures of the church involved. He may have to stand firm for his ideas and convictions, but he should do so after all sides have been considered.

He may learn from the denomination involved. Almost all of the major religious bodies have architectural departments with competent specialists who give counsel and guidance without charge to the church. They do not take the place of an architect, but they give him valuable assistance in making plans that will implement the purposes of the congregation.

He can learn also from the National Council of Churches. Many helpful materials are available at a nominal cost to architects as well as to committees.

4. *Integrity.* Of prime importance in any professional person is the matter of integrity. He must be honest. He must be free from corrupting influences. He must be one who can be trusted, if he is to be an adequate representative of the owner. He will have many opportunities to make decisions in favor of others, but he must remain true to his trust and use all of his talent and influence to manage the project to the best advantage of the owner—the church.

5. *Sympathy.* If a committee had to make a choice between sympathy and talent, it would probably choose in favor of talent. For the architect to be in sympathy with the project, however, is of great value. The building of churches is God's business. Spiritual values are spiritually discerned. Theological views are more easily expressed in art and architecture when deeply held by the artist. This does not mean that the architect must necessarily belong

to the same church or denomination, but it does mean that he should be sincerely earnest in his effort to build the most useful and beautiful building possible. The deeper his sense of mission, the more complete and adequate will be his finished product.

CHOOSING THE MAN

When the committee has finished its investigation, it should select the architect that seems best able to fulfill the requirements and, with the help of the legal subcommittee, formulate a written contract agreement clearly defining the duties and responsibilities of both parties— the owner and the architect. A clear understanding of obligations and privilege at the beginning is essential if unhappiness and disappointment are to be avoided.

When satisfactory agreements have been reached, the committee should recommend to the church that the firm be employed. In some churches, the authority to employ an architect may be delegated to a committee. However, it is quite important, especially in democratic groups, that the whole church enter into the decision. Then the architect is truly the representative of the church and not just the employee of a committee.

THE SELECTION PROCEDURE

The committee may invite for conferences as many architectural firms as are interested in the job. More often, a selected list of prospects will be invited. Interviews with the committee should be unhurried. Each prospect selected should have an opportunity to present his qualifications for consideration of the committee. It is better to take an evening to interview each one than to try to crowd several conferences into one meeting of the committee.

The committee should require from each applicant some biographical information and a list of churches and people for whom he has worked. The wise committee will make careful investigation of each prospect as to his qualifications and his performance in other projects. Great care should be taken to obtain the man best qualified to do this particular job.

WARNINGS TO THE COMMITTEE

Pressures from friends of particular applicants should be resisted. Beware of the man who presents a pretty picture at the beginning. He is not so much interested in solving the problem as getting a job. The best salesman may be one who is least able as an architect. It is usually unwise to be moved by the offers of discounts for professional services. Churches should demand the best service and be willing to pay for it. Piety, although usually a welcome asset, may have little to do with professional ability.

Generally it is unwise for a member of the congregation, however pious and faithful, to serve as architect for his church. He would probably be blamed for whatever mistakes or deficiencies appear after the building is completed. It is well to remember that no one has ever built a perfect building and that someone will be blamed for every error.

DUTIES OF THE OWNER

1. The owner should provide the architect with a copy of the report of the study committee. This report should give a clear picture of present conditions and needs, as well as anticipated needs, of every department of the church. If the survey committee has done its work well, specific needs of the congregation in the areas of worship,

education, fellowship, and administration will be in written form. Supplied with these facts, the architect can determine the problems that he must solve in his drawings.

2. The owner must supply the architect with a complete survey of the property. The survey should include not only the boundaries and dimensions but also a topographical drawing that shows in detail the contour of the land. All easements, restrictions, and other possible impediments or limitations must be indicated. The survey must be certified by a licensed engineer. It must also include grades and lines of streets, alleys, pavements, and adjoining property. The location, dimensions, and character of existing buildings and improvements, including trees, must be reported. The owner is responsible for borings and tests as needed to determine subsoil conditions.

3. Another duty of the owner is to study and make decisions regarding various phases of the services and recommendations of the architect and the committee. At each stage of the process, ample opportunity should be given for the congregation to review the plans and proposals. Formal approval must be given prior to proceeding to the next phase.

4. The owner should give the architect complete information regarding the financial plans. The amount of money available and in prospect is a determining factor in the size and kind of building to be erected. A suburban church of working people engaged an architect who either misunderstood or disregarded the financial limitations of the group. He planned an expensive building far beyond their financial reach. At great expense to the church and some embarrassment to both parties, he was released. Another architect, more sympathetic and cooperative, re-

worked the plans. Without reducing the floor space or the effectiveness of the plan, the cost was reduced $30,000, enabling the project to be completed.

5. After plans are adopted and construction begun, the owner should designate and empower a representative to work with the architect on matters about which decisions must be made without delay. The architect will expect one person to be responsible for conveying any message from or to the owner. This may well be the chairman of the construction committee. The shortest route to chaos would be to permit various members of the congregation to give advice and counsel to the architect during the construction phase.

DUTIES OF THE ARCHITECT

Duties of the architect are set forth by the American Institute of Architects in a standard form of agreement issued in 1961. A summary is presented here. The basic services of the architect are to be performed in four phases.

1. *The Schematic Design Phase.* The architect studies the carefully prepared report of the survey committee which gives the program requirements of each functioning part of the church. He draws a series of sketches showing allocations of space and interrelatedness of the various functions, indicating possible solutions to problems involved. Before an acceptable solution is agreed upon, there may be many such sketches. Repeated conferences with the committees involved are usually needed before all phases of the program are properly provided for and problems of interrelatedness and circulation are solved. All feasible solutions should be presented to the plans committee for consideration.

When agreement is reached, the architect submits to the owner, through the proper committee, a recommendation of the proposed solution and a preliminary estimate of the approximate cost. When the recommendation is approved, he will proceed to the next phase of his work.

The architect should be ready to attend all important meetings of committees and of the congregation to explain his reasoning for suggested solutions.

2. *Design Development Phase.* This second phase of the architect's work builds upon the approved schematic design studies. It develops the project in greater detail. In this part of the process, decisions are made that determine the actual form and character of the building. The kinds of materials to be used, the type of structure to be employed, the type of heating, cooling, and electrical systems must be agreed upon. Various drawings showing the master plan, the over-all development of the whole site, and a colored perspective will help the owner to visualize the finished product. Such drawings are helpful to the publicity committee in conducting an effective public relations program. In this phase, full agreement should be reached on all items, so as to minimize changes that are difficult and expensive to make.

The architect will make another estimate of the probable cost of the building. This estimate may be useful to the finance committee as it works to stimulate giving by the members and to arrange adequate financing for the completion of the project.

3. *The Construction Document Phase.* When phase two has been approved by the owner, detailed working drawings and specifications must be completed. These documents must state the requirements of the building program in exact detail. They must be clear, concise, and

authoritative. They will prescribe the materials, the work-manship, finishes, the mechanical equipment, site development, and whatever information may be required for bidding by contractors. Selected contractors will make their bids from these documents, and the successful bidder will be legally bound to erect the structure as prescribed. Carefully developed plans encourage real competition in bidding and result in a financial saving for the owner.

The architect shall keep the owner informed of any adjustments that may have to be made in cost estimates because of change of market conditions or unavailability of certain materials.

The architect shall be responsible for getting all engineering work done that is necessary for best construction. This will include structural, ventilating, electrical, acoustical, and other necessary engineering services.

The architect shall be responsible for filing the necessary documents and procuring building permits required by governmental agencies having jurisdiction in the particular locality.

4. *The Construction Phase.* The architect shall lend assistance in obtaining the most favorable bid possible. This is facilitated by selection of a group of bidders known to be well qualified. They should have the organization and financial strength needed to finish the task. The architect will normally supervise the opening of the bids and give counsel to the committee in regard to awarding the contract. The architect will assist in preparing the contract between the owner and the builder. During construction he will make decisions on all differences of opinion that might arise between owner and contractor in regard to interpretation of the contract.

As the work progresses, the contractor will make

monthly requests for payment on the work completed. The architect must decide whether the requests are in order and issue necessary certificates for payment.

The architect will check and approve samples of materials and consult with the construction committee regarding any deviations from the specifications that may become necessary because of unavailability of specified materials.

SUPERVISION

The architect should be employed for full service, which includes supervision of the construction. In this capacity he will make visits to the project as needed to evaluate the progress and quality of work to make sure that it proceeds according to agreement. Should he be convinced that the materials or workmanship are inferior, it is his responsibility to require the contractor to make necessary corrections. Such visits will enable the architect to keep the owner informed of the progress of the work. The public relations committee can make good use of such reports as it endeavors to keep the congregation informed and encouraged.

The architect cannot be expected to be a full-time supervisor. Should the project be of sufficient size and significance to demand constant supervision, the owner may, in consultation with the architect, employ a clerk of the works or qualified engineer to give constant supervision.

PAYMENT TO THE ARCHITECT

The amounts and method of payment to the architect should be clearly specified in the contract agreement. Four methods of payment are commonly used.

1. *The percentage method.* The average charge is from 6 to 8 percent of the total cost of the project as determined by the lowest acceptable bid from the contractor. Some variation in rates exists in different parts of the country. Some architects have been known to work for a reduced fee. Church committees should beware of such an offer. They should be willing to pay for the best service, which is the cheapest in the long run.

2. *The fee-plus-cost method.* A fixed fee based on the estimated cost of the building is agreed upon at the beginning. The owner knows exactly what the cost will be. Extra expense incurred because of special requests by the owner will be borne by the owner.

3. *Lump-sum method.* A fixed fee is agreed on by the owner and the architect for whatever services are to be given. This method may be feasible where only partial services are required, such as a specific number of sets of drawings.

4. *The salary method.* This method of payment to the architect is rarely used. A large remodeling project extending over a long period of time may be better served by an arrangement whereby an architect can be called in at any time and paid a monthly salary.

A method of payment should be adopted that will recognize the needs of the architect. He has his own expense and that of his staff. In addition, he must engage structural, mechanical, acoustical, and other engineers to do detailed planning for various aspects of the building. A method recommended by the American Institute of Architects, and usually acceptable, is to pay the architect 15 percent of his anticipated fee at the end of the schematic design phase, and 25 percent on completion of the design development phase. When construction documents, or detail plans and specifications are approved, he may be paid an additional 35 percent. When bids are returned and the contract let, 5 percent more should be paid. This leaves the final 20 percent to be paid during the time of construction, in amounts to be agreed upon.

Because of extra work involved, a larger percentage is charged for planning the remodeling of old buildings. Some architects also expect larger compensation for the planning of residences.

Extra expenses, if any, are paid monthly on the basis of a detailed invoice submitted to the construction committee. If for some reason the work should be discontinued, or the services of the architect no longer be required, he should be paid equitably for the services performed.

Chapter 10

RAISING THE MONEY

VERY FEW CHURCHES have all the cash needed at the beginning of a building program. Special efforts to raise money usually are required. A congregation that does not have to work and sacrifice to build misses the strengthening of fellowship and the deepening of devotion and dedication that comes with struggle. Churches with buildings donated by one or a few, and with considerable endowment support, seldom achieve that spirit of unity and dedication necessary to a great witness.

Because of the great need for funds, church leaders are tempted to use unsatisfactory methods of raising money. Pie suppers, ice-cream socials, oyster stews, rummage sales, and such projects use up energy, raise comparatively little money, and encourage questionable motives for giving. The best source of money for God's work is described in the Bible as "tithes and offerings." The best way to encourage people to give to God's work is to ask them to give it.

THE CAMPAIGN

One method of raising money begins with the finance committee leading the congregation in a "do it yourself" campaign. Members of the church, working with the finance committee, assume all responsibility for planning and directing the effort. Such an effort, successfully, concluded, brings great joy to the congregation. Success in such a campaign requires competent and determined leadership and faithful and cooperative followership. This type of campaign involves the people who are most concerned, and it deepens their love and loyalty to the church. The fee that otherwise might be paid to a fund-raising firm can be applied to program objectives.

There are also disadvantages. An intensive campaign takes an unfair amount of time of many lay leaders and puts too much responsibility on the pastor, who may be forced to neglect his spiritual ministry. There is always the danger that such a campaign will be unsuccessful. If such a campaign is not successful, the people will be reluctant to try it again. Hence, it is important to make the investment of time and money necessary to insure success the first time rather than to risk failure.

A second method is to obtain an outside leader who has been successful in directing financial campaigns. He may be a pastor of another church or he may be a denominational specialist. Most of the denominations have departments of stewardship promotion and are prepared to give assistance to their churches. Some of them may be in a position to provide campaign leaders. The finance committee should by all means obtain financial counsel and advice from its own denominational resources.

A third method, used by an increasing number of churches in recent years, is that of employing professional fund raisers. An organization in this field, The American Association of Fund Raising Counsel, has been developed. When the movement began, some churches strenuously objected to the idea of using "professional" fund-raisers. When they realized, however, that for a long time churches have used professionally trained ministers, educators, musicians, lawyers, and architects, the use of highly skilled leaders in the area of finance seemed less objectionable.

The professional fund-raisers do not solicit pledges. They study the situation and give counsel and advice as to whether the campaign is needed and as to the chances of success. Normally, this preliminary counsel is free if their services are later engaged. The leader carefully analyzes the whole situation. Usually he can indicate fairly accurately how much money will be needed, how much can be raised, and how long it will take to accomplish it. If engaged, he provides experienced leadership in planning the campaign, enlisting and training the workers, and guiding the whole operation.

Whichever method is used in the campaign for money, unless very carefully devised plans follow tested procedures of fund raising, the chances of success will be reduced. The finance committee may need to be enlarged sufficiently to provide for a number of subcommittees. If so, each subcommittee should be assigned special responsibilities for the campaign. The chairmen of the various subcommittees might well become the steering committee to study methods and procedures and give direction to the whole effort. Some of the necessary elements of a successful campaign are:

1. A challenging yet reachable goal. Inexperienced leaders tend to underestimate the giving potential of a congregation.
2. A careful evaluation of the giving ability of each family. A subcommittee that includes some members familiar with individual incomes in the area must evaluate the giving power of each member and potential giver.
3. Someone must be responsible for planning dinner meetings, for refreshments at report meetings, and many other details.

4. Canvassers must be recruited, organized into teams, and adequately trained. In some campaigns, canvassers may be organized so as to give to a select group the potentially large givers. Another group may be responsible for outside givers. The larger contingent of course, will be organized into a sufficient number of teams to see that every member of the church has the opportunity of participating.

5. Attractive printed materials, such as brochures, pamphlets, letters, and news stories, must be produced and properly distributed. This calls for thorough work from a skillful publicity committee. Nothing is more effective than to involve a large number of people in such a meaningful way that they are constantly talking to one another about the progress of the enterprise.

There are definite advantages in having outside expert leadership in a campaign to raise a substantial amount of money for capital improvement. Some of the advantages are:

1. The pastor can give attention to the spiritual needs of his people, which are often made more evident by the strains of a vigorous campaign. Too many pastors have had to carry the load of a sagging financial crusade. Under such a heavy responsibility, they sometimes become the scapegoats for hostility generated in the campaign.

2. Key laymen, who otherwise would have to sacrifice time and energy needed in their businesses or professions, are relieved of a great burden.

3. A trained and experienced leader and trainer of canvassers inspires confidence of the workers—a basic ingredient of success.

4. Precision plans important to victory are made and followed.

5. More money is raised with a competent leader who has spiritual concern and ability to organize and direct.

6. A well-conducted campaign involving a large number of members in service, in sacrificial giving, and in prayer usually results in spiritual revival.

There are a few disadvantages in relying solely on such a campaign to provide funds for church buildings.

1. It delays the time of beginning the construction. Pledges usually are made over 2- or 3-year periods. A church normally would have to wait for many months to accumulate sufficient funds to begin construction.
2. Many members move from the community, leaving pledges unpaid or cancelled. About 20 percent of the people of the United States move every year.
3. Churches made up of small-income families have difficulty raising large sums, especially if a considerable number already are tithers or substantial givers.
4. An extended campaign involving all church leaders will disrupt the regular church program considerably.
5. The cost of the campaign represented by the fee to the directors, plus other administrative expense, may be considerable. In most instances, however, an efficiently directed campaign will bring in much more than the extra cost.

In addition to careful planning and diligent effort, timing is of great importance in a financial campaign. It is never too early to begin raising money. It is not necessary to wait until all plans are made and the details settled. People will give their money if they are convinced of the need and see the direction that the project is going. In fact, some may be discouraged from giving if they are in any way unhappy with some particular part of the detail plan. The best time to raise money is when the congregation feels the need most strongly. At such a time, interest will be at a high level. Fund raising is easier in prosperous times, but a congregation need not wait for better times. During the planning period, when large numbers of the members are involved, and during construction, when the building is becoming a visible reality, is a good time to press for funds.

Deep spiritual motivation is an important ingredient of a successful campaign. As indicated earlier, it is much more important to know why to build than it is to know what to build. The building is not an end in itself; it is only a means of achieving the spiritual objectives of the congregation. Let it be shown that the building is essential to the reconciling work of the church as it seeks to bring the gospel to bear upon human lives. Pledges and gifts then are definitely related, not just to brick and stone, but to the basic purposes of the Kingdom of God.

BORROWING

Seldom will even the most successful campaign raise all the money needed for a building program. It will probably be necessary to borrow some money. Although it is easier today for churches to borrow than it was a few decades ago, banks and other lending agencies are still somewhat hesitant about granting loans to them. One reason for such reluctance is that church buildings are designed for a special purpose and are not easily adapted to other uses. Consequently, there are not many prospective buyers in case of foreclosure. Nor have churches been noted for their efficient business practices. The rapid change of leadership, including pastors, does not enhance efficiency. Normally, church income is entirely from free-will offerings. Another main reason for caution on the part of lending agencies is the fear that ill will may be encouraged among members of the church if foreclosure becomes necessary. But in spite of the extreme caution of money lenders, many church loans are being made.

To increase the chances of getting a suitable loan, a church must give careful attention to financial procedures. The general plan of handling money is of real interest to lenders. The church that uses a good system of book-keeping and reporting, has regular audits, has a financial secretary who receives and deposits the receipts, and a treasurer who disburses the money, both of whom are bonded, will make a good impression.

In seeking a loan, use caution. Seek the advice of some who have had experience. If an application for a loan is refused a few times, the word circulates to lending agencies and the difficulties increase.

Adequate preparation requires a number of items of importance. Be definite about the amount of money needed. To request more than enough is better than to underestimate needs. It is always easier to ask for a reduction than an increase. A clear record of income for ten years will show the church's ability to pay. A complete audit report for the past year may be helpful. The current budget should show estimated sources and proposed distribution of church funds. Demonstrated ability to repay the loan is of more interest to lenders than a first mortgage on the property.

Plans showing what is to be built, along with the architect's estimate of the cost, will be required. The legal description of the property with proof of ownership will be helpful. It is well to have in mind a definite plan for repayment. A complete and businesslike presentation of the application will be appreciated. Lending agencies are also interested in the church leaders. It may be helpful for the committee to ask the pastor to accompany them. His success in the church and his standing in the community and in his denomination may help to get favorable consideration.

WHERE TO BORROW

The larger denominations usually have loan funds, but the demand normally exceeds the supply. Some denominations encourage churches with borrowing power to seek loans from other agencies so that younger and weaker churches without established credit may get their needs supplied. Often denominational loan departments may give helpful advice to finance committees regarding sources of available funds.

Commercial loans are available from many sources. A good place to begin is at the regular bank. Quite probably, the bank will not make a large long-term loan but will be more interested in extending a short-term loan to cover construction costs. One bank may not be able to handle all the loan but may share it with another bank.

A suburban church looking for a sizable loan went to a small, neighborhood bank where the regular account was held. The vice-president politely said that his institution could not render the service requested. During the conversation he casually mentioned a savings and loan association that was not too well known. The finance committee paid little attention to his suggestion and proceeded to canvass the possibilities among the larger companies. After several months of effort, the loan was finally made with the smaller organization mentioned by the local banker at the beginning.

Insurance companies have huge amounts to invest and are increasingly favorable to consideration of church loans. Savings and loan associations lend much money to churches. Foundations in every part of the country are interested in long-term safe investments. Individuals often lend money to churches, but it may not be wise to borrow from a member of the church lest he expect preferential treatment, because of the favor, and seek to wield an undue influence.

LOAN LIMITATIONS

There are some legal limitations to borrowing money. State banking regulations may limit the number of loans to certain kinds of institutions. Lending agencies adopt limitations in order to protect their investments. Some insurance companies will not lend more than 40 to 50 percent of the value of the finished building. Some lenders require personal endorsements by members to secure the loan, but this presents a problem for church members who have to use their credit for their business. The practice of making long-term personal endorsements does offer the advantage of committing men personally to a definite church responsibility.

HOW MUCH TO BORROW

How much should a church borrow? Certainly it is wise to borrow no more than is needed. A church should raise as much cash as possible. The contract with the lender should provide that money be made available only as needed for construction costs. This avoids paying interest on unused borrowed money. A church should not obligate itself in such a way as to jeopardize its credit or to require the curtailment of its regular ministry or mission.

All sorts of suggestions have been made about how much to borrow. Such suggestions may be of some value, but no easy rule of thumb will apply. The strength of the church, the need for the building, and the possibilities of growth must be considered. If larger and better facilities will enable a church to enlist larger numbers of paying members, obtaining a heavy loan for this purpose may be a good step forward. A church can afford to spend what it really needs for expansion if it has the ability to make payments without curtailing its ministries.

CHURCH BONDS

An effective method of raising money for church buildings is termed *income financing,* through which the church issues and sells bonds to investors. This method is used by municipalities, states, and other government units. In recent years it has been widely used by churches. The term *income financing* is derived from the basic principle involved, as stated by one of the pioneers of the movement. He says, "The heart of the income method of financing is that it assigns to a debt-retirement fund account in the bank a sum out of its weekly income sufficient to pay all accruing interest and the principal as and when it becomes due." [1]

To illustrate, a church was meeting in a rented building. A building site had been selected. But how could a young church with no sustained record of giving and no established credit obtain the money for the project during depression years? Income financing was investigated and agreed upon. A bond issue was sold. Within three months the church was meeting in the new building.

Briefly stated, the procedure is as follows:

In a business meeting the church passes a resolution to set up a debt retirement fund account in its own bank. It agrees to deposit into this account out of its first offerings each week, $2.00 for each $1000.0 of the bond issue. It directs the bank to pay such bond on notice, both principal and interest, out of this special account without fur-

[1] J. S. Bracewell, *Building Churches Through Income Financing* (Fresno, California: C.B.F. Press, 1961), p. 70.

ther authorization. The bank agrees to carry the account and to become the paying agent for the bonds.

Having thus provided for the retirement of the debt, the church then issues its notes or bonds in sizes of $50.00, $100.00, $250.00, $500.00, and $1000.00 to be paid by the bank out of the special fund set up by the church. Since the bonds mature at various dates over a period of 14 years, the bank always has on hand funds with which to pay obligations, both principal and interest. Interest coupons are attached to the bonds and paid each six months.[2]

Professional guidance is desirable, but not essential, in launching a bond program. There are definite advantages in engaging the services of one of the many organizations that provide professional guidance in this field. Such advantages are quite similar to those previously discussed in regard to engaging professional fund raisers.

ADVANTAGES OF BOND PLAN

Some advocates of the bond plan are enthusiastic about its advantages, especially to young churches unable to negotiate conventional loans. The strong points are:

1. The rapid growth and movement of the population make it imperative that new churches be established in unprecedented numbers. Usual methods of financing could not meet the need. Income financing offers some hope for the small new church to get a start.

2. Church members, who normally buy most of the bonds, become really involved. Even those with smaller incomes may participate by purchasing bonds of smaller denominations.

3. Bonds require no personal endorsements by mem-

[2] *Ibid.,* pp. 48, 49.

bers, relieving those with financial ability of an unfair share of responsibility.

4. Bonds provide members of the church and other investors with a reasonably safe investment and a larger-than-usual yield.

5. Needed buildings can be erected without waiting for long-term pledges to be paid.

6. The people who use the building will pay for it as they use it.

7. Bonds may be paid off prior to maturity without penalty if the church is able to do it.

8. The cost of a bond plan, even with professional guidance, is considerably less than that of professional fund-raisers, and less than some conventional loans.

9. The property of the church need not be mortgaged to secure the bonds although this is often done.

10. Church bonds are usually a comparatively secure investment since the church's income is pledged to cover them. Churches generally have a more regular and dependable income than many businesses.

11. A growing church can expand its physical facilities as needed by selling additional bonds without first being free of debt.

12. Some denominational organizations have established guarantee funds to secure church bonds. This is in addition to the security offered by the local church. The Illinois Baptist State Association has several hundred thousand dollars in such a fund. Their church bonds have a ready market. In several years of operation this organization has never had to draw on the guarantee fund for a single dollar. Texas Methodists have recently adopted a similar plan.

DIFFICULTIES IN THE BOND PLAN

Although the bond plan offers a number of advantages, some difficulties should be noted:

1. The church may not be able to sell enough bonds to complete the project. This will delay the building program and discourage the members. A good answer is to obtain the services of a professional who will guarantee the sale of the total issue.

2. The bond plan is not suited for every church. Smaller churches with more modest programs usually have better success with the bond plan.

3. Where lay leadership is not adequate, the pastor may have to take up the burden of promotion and sale of bonds.

Chapter 11

OTHER IMPORTANT COMMITTEES

PRECEDING CHAPTERS have highlighted major functions of certain special committees a congregation needs at crucial points throughout the planning and execution stages of a comprehensive program of real estate acquisition and development. The purpose of this chapter is to bring into proper focus some principal responsibilities and duties of four other important committees: the legal committee, the construction committee, the furniture committee, and the publicity committee. So significant are these committees that the effectiveness of their work can almost "make or break" the whole project.

THE LEGAL COMMITTEE

Any church in the process of acquiring and developing real estate should be properly organized for making business transactions that require legal knowledge and discernment. The legal subcommittee of the building committee is responsible for safeguarding the church's interests in such matters. This group need not consist of more than four or five members, but it should be very carefully chosen. Willingness to seek needed legal counsel is one of the most important qualifications of members of this committee.

Incorporation of a church is not absolutely necessary but certainly should be seriously considered. An incorporated church, being a legal entity, may buy or sell property, enter into contracts, sue and be sued, and otherwise act before the law as an individual, subject to the charter granted by the state in which the church is based.

"Most local religious societies are in their origin merely voluntary associations, and as such are neither capable of taking grants of land nor of suing in their own name, since that name is unrecognized by law." [1]

When after colonial times the church ceased to be a part of the political community, corporate powers were granted to the pastor and later to trustees selected for the purpose. Now, the congregation itself may be incorporated and trustees elected with powers only to carry out the specific instructions of the congregation.

Many churches develop by-laws that prescribe the ways by which the congregation may make decisions. In some denominations such matters are provided for in official church discipline or standard polity. However, many independent churches have never agreed upon a uniform way of handling business affairs.

To avoid confusion and misunderstanding, business should be transacted only at times specified in the by-laws. Duties and responsibilities of officers should be clearly delineated. Serious problems during a major expansion project could be avoided by adopting in advance businesslike procedures that are clearly stated and fully understood.

[1] N. F. Brand and Y. M. Ingram, *The Pastor's Legal Adviser* (Nashville: Abingdon-Cokesbury Press, 1942), p. 49.

REAL ESTATE

A major responsibility of the legal committee is that of guiding the church in regard to real estate transactions. If a new site is to be acquired, the legal committee should be instructed to proceed with the purchase of the land. If it is vacant land, the identity of the owner may not be readily available. A search of the courthouse records will need to be made. If several owners of small plots must be dealt with in order to obtain a larger area for expansion, caution should be taken in the approach. Prices have been known to rise suddenly when an owner feels that the prospective purchaser is a bit anxious. A good procedure is to enlist the help of a reputable real estate agent who will quietly get all the facts and help plot the course most likely to succeed in the purchase. The legal committee must provide for a thorough investigation of the title to make sure that there are no encumbrances or limitations.

TITLE

The proposed site should be surveyed. The fence may be on the neighbor's land. A careful examination may reveal an old, forgotten mortgage, tax lien, or an unpaid assessment for sewer or paving. A dedicated but undeveloped street may cut across the plot. A congregation purchased a new site in a rapidly growing subdivision. Afterward, an examination of the title revealed the fact that a pipeline easement had been granted to an oil company years before. The easement did not cloud the title, but it prescribed to some extent where the buildings could be located, since the agreement permitted no structure to be placed over the pipeline.

Two methods are used to assure a clear title, free from defects.

1. The purchaser may require a title search and an abstract of the title. This is a written history of the property's title as disclosed by public records. A title attorney should review the abstract and give an opinion of the title. This does not guarantee, however, that the title is free from defects. It deals only with items that are a matter of public record. Title defects not included in the public record could cause trouble. Some of them are: an undisclosed spouse, forgery, deeds delivered after death, missing heirs, improper interpretation of wills, and deeds signed by minors or incompetent persons.

2. The purchaser may obtain title insurance. A title owner's policy, available in every state, assures that the purchaser will be protected if any title defect appears. All costs in defending the title are covered. The owner also is covered in case of the loss of the property up to the limits of the policy.

RESTRICTIONS

Restrictions are sometimes written into the deeds. Residences only may be allowed. These may be limited to certain types and sizes. A church may not assume that these limitations do not apply because courts have held that the lofty purposes of a religious organization do not give it a right to set at naught covenants any more than other institutions.

State laws vary a great deal in treatment of churches in regard to such matters. The best thing is for the legal committee to get clearance in advance on any possible condition that may interfere with the plans.

Extra caution should be taken in regard to donated real estate. Often the owner is willing to donate the use of the property to a church but will stipulate that if and when the land ceases to be used for church purposes, title will revert to the owner. In such a case the donor is the legal owner. The title is not conveyable. Since the property cannot be mortgaged, no loan can be made to further the building program. After using property for years, many churches have found such restrictive terms a burden.

ARCHITECT

The legal committee may be given the responsibility for formalizing the contractual agreement with the architect. The terms of such contracts are fairly uniform, especially among members of the American Institute of Architects (see Chapter 9). Local conditions, however, may call for deviations from the norm in regard to fees and to services. The legal committee must be fully informed so as to give the church the best possible service.

CONTRACTOR

Agreements with the contractor are of great importance. Here contracts should be executed in great detail and with extreme care. The contractor agrees to erect a building of a specific nature on a particular piece of land for certain considerations, usually money. The detailed plans and specifications prepared by the architect and his engineers are normally a part of the contract and must be followed exactly except for essential changes that can be made only with the permission of the architect. The contract specifies a date for completion of the building and often prescribes a penalty for any delay beyond the agreed-upon completion date.

The owner agrees to pay the agreed-upon price when the work is completed. Normally, the contract provides for regular payments for the work as it is being completed. The architect and the construction committee usually determine how much work has been completed and how large a payment is due the contractor each month.

A competent architect is qualified to draw up a contract between the owner and the contractor, but he is not a lawyer, and in some states may be prevented from rendering this service. The legal committee should advise with him regarding this most important agreement.

INSURANCE COVERAGE

Because of legal involvements, the matter of insurance coverage during the building program may well be the responsibility of the legal committee. The protection afforded by many types of insurance is more important during a major expansion program than at any other time. Finances already under great strain because of the project could hardly stand a calamitous event.

Although reputable contractors usually provide most of the essential coverage, this should be verified by the committee. The cost should be included in the bid price. When the church decides to serve as its own contractor, the committee should see that the necessary protection is provided. Court judgments in liability cases are much larger than in former years. Many types of insurance coverage are available. Someone must choose what will be needed to protect the interests of the congregation. The following list (partial) of types of insurance that may be needed has been suggested by the Architecture Department of the Sunday School Board, Southern Baptist Convention, Nashville, Tennessee, and is used here by permission.

INSURANCE NEEDED WHILE BUILDING

Workmen's Compensation—protects the church and provides money for injured employees who can't work. Since state laws vary on this point, it will be necessary for the committee to familiarize itself with legal requirements and see that the coverage is sufficient and in line with local conditions.

Some churches will already have this on regular employees. The insuring company will be glad to extend coverage to those who will be working during a construction program.

Social Security—is another type of coverage applying to those employed by a church. If the church serves as its own contractor, those employed should be covered in accordance with the law governing this; proper payments and records must be turned into the Government revenue authorities. If the job is let by contract, it is the responsibility of the construction firm to handle this.

Comprehensive General Liability—defines a type of insurance to protect the contractor and church against damages to the public and property by the contractor or his employees. Several items should be included in this phase of the insurance: (1) bodily injury; (2) property damage; and (3) contractual, which protects the subcontractors. Careful consideration should be given to the advisability of extending the "property damage" coverage to include adjacent or other property that could be involved in a loss due to negligence on the part of the contractor; likewise, it should be kept in mind that existing property or buildings of the church may be entrusted to the contractor for his use during construction, and possible extended coverage would be desired for these.

Comprehensive Automobile Liability—would protect against bodily and property damage by vehicles driven or used by the contractor's employees during the building process.

Owner's Protective Liability—describes an extended coverage to protect the church in event some claim should be filed against it as owner, because of conditions aggravated by the contractor. Occasionally suits are brought against the owner of a project rather than the contractor.

Builder's Risk Insurance—is intended for protection to all parties having an interest in the work. In brief, it covers a number of items such as loss by fire; extended coverage (windstorm, hail, explosion, riot, civil commotion, aircraft, vehicles, smoke, and so forth); vandalism and malicious mischief.

Earthquakes, hurricanes, and floods are not common to all parts of the country, but these can be insured against, when and wherever needed.

This coverage usually increases as the building operation progresses. Likewise, it terminates at such time as the building is completed, and the committee should be careful to see that the regular insurance program of the church is put into effect at the proper time to give the church continuous protection.

Loss of Use—consideration should be given to the fact that sometimes the church can be caused the inconvenience of losing use of a building in event of an accident. Not only is this true during a construction period, but it would also apply to the regular insurance program. If such coverage is desired, it should be included in the policies.

Guaranty Bonds—although not always considered as insurance should be included in the contracts. The church should require the contractor to furnish bond covering the faithful performance of the contract and the full payment of all obligations related thereto. NOTE: If such bond is required by instructions given previous to the submission of bids, the premium shall be paid by the contractor; if subsequent thereto, it shall be paid by the owner. [Illustration: A church in a western state was about one-half completed when the contractor was forced to quit because of financial failure. The bonding company employed a supervisor and carried the project to completion. The church was protected from great loss.]

The church, as owner of the construction project, is liable, and consequently responsible, for arranging adequate protection for all concerned in cases of bodily injury, including death, which may arise from operations.

One other item closely related to insurance during a building program is coverage on residences or other buildings purchased and used temporarily for church purposes. The insuring company should be notified of the "church use" of such a building so there can be no doubt as to the coverage.

Whatever portion of this expense is to be borne by the church, should be anticipated and included as a portion of the building cost. Remember, it is better to have it and not need it than to need it and not have it.

THE CONSTRUCTION COMMITTEE

The basic purpose of this committee is to see that the church gets the building that was planned and authorized —to make sure that what was bought is delivered. The committee works closely with the architect, who is the master builder. The members of the committee are his advisors, but he goes to the contractor with any questions or suggestions on their behalf. To avoid misunderstanding, only one person (usually the chairman) has authority to speak for the committee.

The contractor may not be familiar with the polity of the church he is serving. The committee is able to help him understand why some things have to be done in particular ways. The contract may also insist that he be protected from interference by any member or members of the church. Some builders require a signed agreement to this effect. If such a procedure is required, the committee interprets to the church the reasons for it. Church members are prone to visit the job and may often interfere with workers, damage the construction, or possibly injure themselves.

CHOOSING A CONTRACTOR

The first important duty of the committee is to choose the contractors to bid on the job. There is danger in permitting any and all to bid on a project of considerable size. If church members do not understand why bidding is restricted to a few firms, the construction committee should help them understand. A number of firms in almost every locality do various types of construction work. Many are not qualified to build the type of building planned. Some firms do not have the organization needed to complete the work on time. Others may not be assured of sufficient financial resources. Another may have a history of labor difficulties that may jeopardize the effort. Usually it is not wise for a member of the church to bid on the job. If he bids higher than a nonmember, some will feel that he was not being fair with the congregation. If he gets the job, any mistake or disagreement may cause hard feelings and disturb the fellowship of the church.

With the help of the architect, the construction committee should select a list of contractors who have a reputation for reliability and efficiency. Those selected should have resources to do the job and should be able to provide performance bonds that will guarantee it. Each firm on the list should be given a copy of the plans and specifications to use in determining the cost of the building and a bidding price. From two to four weeks will be needed for preparation of bids.

The architect and the committee may feel that it is also important to prepare an approved list of subcontractors to bid on some of the more important aspects of the

building. If separate bids are taken from selected subcontractors, these bids should be incorporated into the
general contract.

CHOICE OF MATERIALS

The construction committee works with the architect
in choosing materials and equipment. If the specified
items are not available immediately, this committee must
decide whether to wait or to choose a substitute. Changes
in plans are sometimes necessary but they are expensive.
The contractor usually adjusts his price to take care of
them. It is much better to do a careful job of planning
and permit no changes after plans have been agreed upon.
But this cannot always be done. An authorized group
must make the decisions for the church.

PAYMENT

As the construction progresses, the contractor is entitled to payments covering the work completed. The
architect receives the request for payment and, after
satisfying himself that the work has been done, recommends to the construction committee that payment be
made. The committee then authorizes payment by the
treasurer.

AFTER COMPLETION

When the building is completed it must be inspected
and accepted by the owner before final payment is made
to the contractor. The logical procedure is for the construction committee to inspect the building and make recommendations to the building committee. If the finished
product is acceptable, the building committee, if authorized to do so, may receive it for the church. Otherwise,
the building committee recommends to the congregation

that the building be received. If any part of the work is unacceptable, funds due the contractor may be withheld until the questionable work is corrected.

The work of the construction committee may continue beyond the completion of the building. In normal procedure, the building is guaranteed for one year by the contractor. If defects appear in materials or workmanship during the period of the guarantee, the construction committee, in cooperation with the architect, gets the deficiency corrected.

THE FURNITURE COMMITTEE

The more comfortable and adequate the furniture, the more effective the functioning of the whole program. The furniture committee, therefore, must be thoroughly familiar with all the church activities and must be capable of careful and detailed planning. Its first responsibility is to see that the probable cost of the furniture is anticipated and planned as a part of the cost of the building. It is not uncommon, however, for churches to build well but to use up all available monetary resources in the process, leaving little or nothing for furniture. Of course, the exact amount required for furniture cannot be determined beforehand, but a working estimate can be made.

DETAILED STUDY

The furniture needs of every department and activity should be considered from the first. Better prices are usually available with larger orders or contracts. Churches often find that more money than they had expected can be raised or borrowed. If sufficient resources are not available to do a complete job, purchase of certain items can be deferred.

Detailed lists of all furniture not to be installed as a part of the building must be made early. If the project is of considerable size, the committee cannot make a hurried list of needed items without risking involvement of the church in bad choices, needless delays, and extra expense.

WORSHIP CENTER

Pews and pulpit furniture should be beautiful, comfortable, and permanent. These will generally be designed to fit the size and architecture of the worship center. This means that decisions must be made and orders placed six to eight months before the building is to be completed. Choir and balcony seats should be chosen to harmonize with the interior design. They should be chosen not for beauty alone but also for comfort and durability. Church furniture manufacturers estimate that pews and chancel furniture usually cost from 5 to 10 percent of the cost of the building, depending on the architectural style and quality desired.

EDUCATION BUILDING

In the religious education program, every department will need different items with various dimensions to fit the size and function. Chairs and tables must be ordered according to dimensions appropriate for the particular age group. Comfort and durability should be of great concern. Because such items are subject to frequent moves, the church should not try to economize by purchasing less durable ones. Ten to 15 percent of the cost of an education building may be needed for furniture. Large school-supply houses may offer the best materials and the best bids on tables, chairs, and blackboards. A better choice of office furniture and fixtures may be found in large firms that specialize in such equipment.

WHOM TO CONSULT

The committee will need to obtain information and counsel from many sources, which should include, by all means, the leading workers in the various departments of the church. Neighboring churches that have recently built may share their experience. For most churches, the denomination headquarters can suggest the names of reliable manufacturers and dealers as prospective bidders. Being acquainted with the particular approach to worship and religious education, denominational officers usually can furnish a list of the most suitable kinds and sizes of materials needed for every department. The Church Furniture Manufacturing Association in a pamphlet makes the following suggestions about purchase agreements:[1]

Any agreement to purchase church furniture should set forth clearly all essential elements of the transaction, including:

1. Name and address of buyer
2. Terms of payment
3. Conditions of sale
4. A complete description of the product including catalog numbers, material, color, and specific reference to a seating plan if installation constitutes a part of the agreement.
5. Total amount of purchase with any applicable sales, consumer, use, or other similar taxes separated.
6. Information as to when delivery is to be expected, and the f.o.b. point of delivery

[1] A *Guide: Considerations in the Purchase of Church Furniture* (published as a service to churches by: The Church Furniture Manufacturers Association, A Division of National Association of Furniture Manufacturers, 666 North Lake Shore Drive, Chicago 11, Illinois).

7. The nature and extent of the responsibility of each of the parties for installation

Delivery dates are of great importance. The buyer should inform the supplier as to delivery date desired and notify him in case of necessary changes. Should the supplier be unable to meet the date specified, he must so inform the buyer.

MAKING CHOICES

In every section of the country can be found manufacturers or suppliers who will be willing to demonstrate their products to prospective buyers. The committee, in order to save time, might arrange for two demonstrations in one evening. If several demonstrations are desired, more time must be arranged, during either the day or another evening.

The manufacturer or supplier is under obligation to disclose all pertinent facts about the composition of his product. He should specify the particular kind and grade of wood or material used. If plywood or other fabricated materials are used, this should be clearly indicated. If samples are provided, it is the responsibility of the manufacturer to provide a sample of the regular design and quality that will be furnished or to point out clearly how the sample differs from the item to be furnished.

Better pews may be procured by inviting bids from several suppliers. Especially in regard to pews and pulpit furniture, prices should include complete installation with a satisfactory warranty.

THE PUBLICITY COMMITTEE

Much of what a church accomplishes depends on the image it projects. Every church gets publicity whether it is planned or unplanned, good or bad. Jesus attracted crowds whenever "it was noised abroad that he was in the house." (Mark 2:1.) Publicity cannot be avoided. A committee is needed to insure the right kind of publicity and to increase the amount of it. The committee should be well informed about all the activities of the church. The chairman of the committee should also be a member of the building council so that he may have complete knowledge of what every subcommitte is doing. The committee should prepare for its responsibility by defining its purposes and by studying the technique and means of good publicity.

PURPOSE

The basic purpose of the publicity committee is to keep the membership of the church informed about the work of each subcommittee and the progress of the whole undertaking. Many problems and misunderstandings are avoided when people know the facts. Doubts and suspicions arise where there is lack of information. When people are interested and inspired, a high level of cooperation is possible. The raising of money for the project can be greatly stimulated by the work of a good publicity committee. The challenge before this committee is to create and maintain a reservoir of understanding and goodwill for the message and mission of the church.

PUBLICS

In planning its work, the committee should identify its publics. Of primary concern are the members of the church, of which there are several groups. Some are directly involved in the work of the committee. Others are vitally interested. Some have little or no interest, and possibly a few are in active opposition. The committee is challenged to get the message to all these groups in such a way as to stimulate the largest possible participation.

The local community is an important public. Every church is interested to some extent in what other churches are doing. Information should be shared. Of greater concern to the committee should be the community's unchurched and unenlisted. While a building is being planned and erected is a good time to try to get their attention and interest, and, if possible, their involvement. For those who are definitely prospects for membership a more direct approach may be taken through the mail. Letters and brochures explaining what the new facilities and the new approaches will be may be the means of winning new members.

MEDIA

The property itself offers one of the best means of publicity. Everyone is interested in new buildings under construction. A large sign on the site, giving pertinent facts about the building and possibly the expanded program, will be read and may kindle considerable anticipation. The weekly bulletin, if well done, is read by those attending worship services. Many churches send newsletters to the homes of all members. Regular announcements and articles of interest should appear in these church papers.

Newspapers are interested in religious news because people, their readers, are interested. To get articles into newspapers, especially the larger ones, requires special understanding of newspaper procedures. Their definition of "news" should be understood. Newspapers must make money. Hence, "news" to newspapers is what people will pay money to read. Items dealing with the unusual, the odd, and the spectacular are usually more acceptable.

Fairly common events that have a unique angle or are connected with a colorful personality can often be made into good newspaper material. The names and activities of status people are nearly always considered newsworthy.

If the committee hopes to get free newspaper publicity, it should plan for several stories, possibly with pictures of significant events, to be released at appropriate times. Help of an experienced writer should be sought in preparing such articles.

Some helpful hints in working with newspapers are: get acquainted with the editor or the religious reporter; honor deadlines; recognize that brevity and accuracy are important; look for something unique and unusual; give the name and phone number so that the editor may conveniently call for additional information.

Although the county newspaper, usually a weekly, may accept religious articles more readily than will large dailies, the same courteous procedures in working with the editor should apply. In suburban areas advertising weeklies are quite numerous. These papers usually are distributed free to all residents of a community. They are more interested in local cultural and religious activity than in more spectacular events. These papers are read by a relatively large number of residents and may be quite helpful to the publicity committee.

With the possible exception of the pastor's personality, the church building itself is the most important subject for publicity. Personalities on the building committee offer opportunities for articles. Names of people, especially if they are readers, are most acceptable to newspapers. Other events that may be exploited for publicity are:

Selection of the architect
Adoption of floor plans

Approval of elevation drawing
Letting of contract
Groundbreaking
Cornerstone laying
Putting on the steeple
Accepting the building
Dedication service
Burning of the note

In publicizing such events, the committee should plan for stories and releases at the proper time. Care should be taken to space the efforts so that there will be no lag. The temptation may be to overpublicize at the beginning, instead of building to a climax at the proper time.

The committee may decide to prepare an attractive brochure showing a picture of the building as it will appear upon completion and describing new ministries and services to be provided. Movies and slides showing the progress, as well as interesting aspects of the construction, will arouse interest—especially among members. These could be shown to various groups in their meetings and could be taken to the homes of interested shut-ins. A file of photographs and movies showing the building in the various stages of construction may be of interest to the generations that follow.

CHURCH PARSONAGES

TRADITIONALLY, CHURCHES have assumed the responsibility of providing a home for the pastor. Until modern times there might have been good reasons for the persistence of this custom. Inadequate transportation and communication made it important for the pastor to live near the church. Short-term pastorates made it inadvisable for a pastor to own a home. Small salaries often prevented the pastor from owning a home comparable to that of others in the community. The lack of staff personnel left only the pastor to look after the business of the church.

Times have changed, however. Such conditions no longer exist in most churches. The time is past due for an objective evaluation of the whole concept of church-owned parsonages, with the intention of doing what is best for the church and the pastor.

There are evidences of a strong trend away from the custom. A seminary student in Louisville, Kentucky, made a survey of approximately one hundred pastors. Seventy percent of the pastors lived in church-owned homes. Sixty percent preferred that the church provide the parsonage. It is significant, however, that 40 percent of the preachers involved would prefer to own their homes. This is indica-

153

tion of a strong trend. W. D. Powell says,[1] "The parsonage is a thing of the past. It served well in its time, but that time has passed. Today, there is a new generation of men who want to render service on a more permanent basis."

Every church should carefully study all sides of this question. In the following paragraphs are several important considerations. First, let us consider some arguments in favor of the pastor owning his home.

1. Leadership in the churches will be more stable if the pastor owns his own home. The rapid turnover in pastorates is a scandal in some denominations. The average term of office is reported to be less than three years. Formerly, when the emphasis was more strongly on a preaching ministry, length of tenure was not as important as it is now. The increasing demand for a person-centered ministry, makes it extremely important that the pastor stay longer, so that he may know his people well.

2. When the pastor owns his home he will be encouraged to commit himself more effectively to a program of community development. His moral and spiritual leadership can be strengthened because his roots will be deeper in the community. He will feel more like making long-range plans for the church and its ministry.

3. Members of the family may be happier and more stable if they live in their own home. A house can be obtained that will fit the needs of a particular family. The sex, the age, and the number of children in the family can be considered. Many pastors' wives have a difficult time trying to fit the furniture they have into the house the church has provided. Important also is the need for the pastor to live in a house that fits his income. Many

[1] W. D. Powell, "Ministers Can Own Their Own Homes." *Church Management,* June, 1960, p. 60.

church parsonages are obsolete, too large for a modern family, difficult to heat and impossible to cool.

The children of the pastor may be more deeply rooted. No one can estimate the emotional damage done to millions of youngsters who are being constantly uprooted and moved. And too, a location may be chosen that will take into account social and educational opportunities that fit the family needs.

4. The pastor may be better off financially. It is assumed that if a pastor owns his home the church will provide a housing allowance. The wise pastor will use this sum and possibly some of his salary to build an equity in residential real estate. When changing fields of service or upon retirement, some resources would be available to provide housing for the pastor and his family. The usual retirement income of clergymen hardly provides sufficiently for house payments or even rental charges for comfortable living.

5. The church may also be better off financially to provide a housing allowance instead of a house. Twenty-five thousand dollars invested in a residence uses up capital funds or credit that might be needed badly for the expansion of plant facilities. The cost to the church is considerable. Twenty-five thousand dollars at 6 percent equals $1,500 per year. In addition, there are insurance, upkeep and repair, the customary remodeling and redecorating that comes with each change of pastors, and in some states, taxes. When normal depreciation is added to these other expenses, the church may find it financially profitable to give the pastor an adequate housing allowance instead of to own the parsonage.

The question of who should own the house in which the pastor lives is similar to most other questions in that it has more than one side. Now let us consider some of the arguments that can be made for church-owned parsonages.

1. The church can determine where the pastor will live. A home near the church and the center of the community makes the pastor more available to many of the members. There was a time when accessibility was most important. Now, however, with telephones and rapid transportation, proximity is not a prime consideration.

2. The church may be able to provide a much finer home than the pastor could buy. For prestige purposes, some churches may feel that this is important. It is true that many pastors have enjoyed living in far better homes than they could ever afford to purchase. The wisdom of such procedure is open to question. In many churches, such living would provide a barrier between some members of the church and their pastor. And, too, when retirement time comes, the pastor and family might have to make a radical adjustment in living habits.

3. In supplying the comforts and conveniences of a good home, a church has the opportunity of expressing love and appreciation to the pastor and his family.

4. In providing the house, a church may build an equity in—and someday own—a permanent parsonage. This may be good procedure, but it does not necessarily mean a saving. The purchase price invested would return in interest a sizable part of a housing allowance.

LOCATION OF THE PARSONAGE

Assuming that the church decides to provide a home instead of an allowance for the pastor, a careful study must be made as to location, size and arrangement of the residence.

First, let us consider the location. The pastor's home should not be located on the church site. Most churches are cramped for building and parking space. To build a residence on valuable ground needed for expansion of plant facilities is unjustifiable. Many churches trying to expand to meet the needs of a growing constituency have found the parsonage taking up space where a new education building ought to be.

There are other disadvantages to such closeness. The pastor and family become more easily the victims of canvassers, beggars, and casual visitors. There may be too much use of the pastor's home by the church. The church location is often at the hub of community traffic and business which is not the most desirable place for a residence. When built to harmonize with the church plant, the home becomes out of date and out of style in one generation. It is too good to tear down and impossible to sell or exchange.

There are, however, a few advantages in having the parsonage and church building together. It is easily recognized as a part of the church property. Together, the buildings may make a greater impact on the community. The pastor may be able to see more people and render more personal service. The home is easily reached between meetings. Maintenance of buildings and grounds would be simpler and cheaper.

Although it seems less desirable to build the home and church building together on one plot, there are good reasons for locating the parsonage within easy walking distance of the church. It may make two cars unnecessary. The wife and children could attend meetings without the preacher having to furnish transportation. The wife may also have the use of the car while the husband is working at the church. The pastor's home should be close enough to be easy to find and convenient for those who may need him.

A residence located among others is more easily sold if the church should want to change the parsonage or its policy regarding the pastor's housing. It is usually wiser to build new homes in newer areas where values will remain at a higher level for a longer period of time. If a loan must be secured to build the house, the location should enhance the investment. A lending agency would hardly be interested in providing the money for a home to be built near a church or a business, or in a section of the city where other property is deteriorating. The resale value should always be considered.

Wise planning will take into account the character of the community and the possibility of a changing social situation. The matter of convenience to stores, schools, and transportation facilities is important. Fire and police protection, street lighting, garbage collection, and other services need to be considered. Parks and community recreation facilities are a godsend at times.

ARRANGEMENTS OF THE HOME

A church planning to build a parsonage should appoint a committee that will give serious study to the functions of the home. Will the house be used for socials, weddings, and other meetings involving a large number of people? Will the pastor be expected to entertain visiting speakers and other guests of the church? If the parsonage is to be an installation that will be used for a long time, plans should be made to care for all contingencies. A future pastor may have a much larger family than the present one. It would be better and cheaper to anticipate such needs now than to build an extension later.

The committee should get the help of an architect. Ready-made plans are available from some denominational agencies, catalogs, and newspapers at a nominal cost. Since the services of an architect will be needed to insure the proper foundation for the soil conditions and to conform to building code requirements, why not get his professional help from the beginning? Costly mistakes may be avoided. He will know how to locate the residence on the plot to protect against winter winds and summer sun, to take advantage of prevailing breezes and the best view. To do a quality job, any committee will need the help of a professional—the architect.

THE STUDY

A room designated as a study is of prime importance. Located near the front of the house, it is easily accessible to visitors who come for business or for counseling. Couples desiring to talk with the pastor about wedding plans or marital problems will find it convenient to come together here in the evening. The privacy afforded by such a room will be appreciated. Church officers and committees may need to talk to the pastor alone. With a quiet place to work in the home, the pastor can make use of bits of time for study in the late evening or early morning hours without disturbing normal family life. Since a pastor is never off duty, he needs a place to work at home as well as at church.

The study should be accessible from the foyer and the living room, which could double as a waiting room. It should be protected from traffic and sounds from the rest of the house. A closet and bookshelves are required. A fireplace and other appointments to convey warmth will make it more effective. At least a half-bath should be nearby or adjacent to the room. With a comfortable davenport or couch, the study could be used as an emergency sleeping room.

LIVING ROOM

The size of the living room should be determined by its anticipated uses. Normally, it should be large enough for some receptions, small weddings, and other social functions. The church that plans to make such use of its parsonage, should provide rugs, drapes, and other essential furnishings. These are expensive items that may not fit the next parsonage in which the pastor must live.

Many modern churches are equipped with chapels and areas for entertaining small groups. Where such is the case, the parsonage living room may be smaller and less expensive. Care should be taken to locate doors and windows so that large wall areas will be available for furniture. The parsonage should be planned so as to avoid the necessity of using the living room as a passageway to the upstairs or other rooms.

DINING ROOM

The dining room should join the living room but should be separable by some means so that privacy during the meals is ensured. It should be easily accessible from the kitchen. If the dining area is an integral part of the living room, as in so many modern homes, a breakfast room large enough for family meals should be provided.

KITCHEN

The kitchen should be close to the front entrance but not visible from the entrance foyer. It should be just large enough to be efficient. An oversized kitchen requires hundreds of extra steps. Since the pastor's wife, in many respects, has two jobs, modern labor-saving devices are a good investment for the church. Young mothers are grateful for kitchen windows that give a convenient view of the playground.

BEDROOMS

The average family needs at least three bedrooms. These should be of adequate size, not miniature, and should have plenty of closet and storage space. If the church expects visiting speakers and other guests to be housed in the parsonage, a fourth bedroom should be provided. Churches increasingly are providing hotel entertainment for their guests. This usually is more satisfactory to the visitors and avoids putting an extra burden on the pastor's family. Unless the home is air-conditioned, bedrooms should be located so as to avoid the heat of the sun and to acquire the best natural ventilation.

FAMILY ROOM

The family room is a most welcome innovation in residence planning, especially for the parsonage. Here a pastor's family can relax and feel human without mussing up the living room, which needs to be tidy at all times. Children can do their homework or possibly watch the favorite T.V. program without interfering with a conference or a wedding that may be taking place in the front part of the house. Space and furniture for informal meals is often provided in this room.

CHURCH ENCAMPMENTS

A SIGNIFICANT NEW trend in the development of church facilities is the rapid increase in the number of church encampments. The camp meetings of the nineteenth century, which were held in groves, tents, or other temporary places, have gone.

Instead, since the early part of the twentieth century, tabernacles, cabins, and dormitories of a permanent type have appeared in ever increasing numbers. Such facilities are variously called camps, assemblies, conferences, retreats, and encampments. These terms are often used interchangeably. Sometimes they refer to types of programs conducted as well as to places where people gather. The word *encampment* is used here because it definitely indicates a place where people camp or assemble.

Since the 1920's, the increase in the number of such establishments, as well as the amount of money invested in them, is amazing. As early as 1947, Dr. Paul H. Vieth, noting this rapid development, said, "It is possible that the camp and conference program which has grown with such amazing speed in the last quarter of a century will prove to be as powerful an agency of Christian education in our day as the Sunday School came to be in another generation." [1]

[1] Paul H. Vieth, *The Church and Christian Education* (St. Louis, Missouri: The Bethany Press, 1947), p. 129.

Encampments are not being developed by individual churches but by councils of churches, synods, associations, conferences, and conventions. Baptists in one southern state have more than thirty encampments that are owned and operated by associations and groups of associations. Many of these establishments permit individual churches to own and develop their own property on the site. Others permit individual churches to use some of the facilities for a nominal charge, thereby rendering a distinct service. In some other areas, however, this is not permitted because of a strong feeling that all facilities should be owned and operated by one authority and under the control of a manager or board. Such a plan makes it easier to avoid conflicting interests and to eliminate activities that do not further the basic purposes of the encampment.

TYPES OF ENCAMPMENTS

In earlier days the whole family was involved in the camp meetings. Modern camps may be typed or classified by groups served. There are boys', girls', junior high, senior high, youth, or men's camps. They may be classified by the time involved, such as weekend, one week, or all summer. The earliest camps were for boys and youth groups and, for the most part, used rough facilities.

The recent trend is to plan and build more comfortable facilities to care for the whole family and for many groups. In some areas, meetings that attract the whole family are called assemblies. The term *conference* is also used for such gatherings as well as for meetings of particular groups with more specialized interests. Retreats, which are becoming more and more popular, usually involve a smaller number of people especially concerned about deepening the spiritual life. Often a variety of meetings and programs are in progress at the same time.

Encampment planners and developers may well consider providing suitable equipment to care for all such meetings.

GETTING STARTED

These establishments may get started in a number of ways. Many have been started with very little advance thinking as to the needs for such an undertaking. Some have been begun because of the gift of a site. At first this may seem to be a magnificent gesture. However, unless an encampment is needed and the site is adequate in size and in the proper location, this seeming generosity may in time prove to be a major handicap.

Some camps have been inaugurated because of the influence of an interested individual. Others have been started in an effort merely to keep up with other groups or denominations having such a program or facility.

It is possible to start an encampment and to develop, along the way, a philosophy and procedures that become effective. Such is not the ideal way, however.

IDEAL WAY

The ideal way to start an encampment is to begin with a study committee. Such a committee should be representative of all the groups concerned. It should seek complete answers to several basic questions and present them in a report to the sponsoring group. Some questions to be answered are:

Why have an encampment?
What areas and ages should it serve?

What capacity should it be?
How much will it cost?
Who will provide the money?
Who will set operation policies?
What are the prospects for future usefulness?

When such questions are thoroughly explored and a decision is made to proceed with the establishment of an encampment, still other considerations must be grappled with before work can begin.

Where should the encampment be located?
Is the water supply adequate?
Can utilities be provided?
What buildings will be needed?
Who will draw the plans?
What type of construction?
What activities will be provided for?
Which buildings will be constructed first?

Answers to these questions should be based on a philosophy of camping and a clear statement of the purposes and objectives of the undertaking.

PURPOSES AND OBJECTIVES

The predetermined purposes and objectives of the encampment should guide in planning the program, in selecting the site, and in constructing the buildings. In general, camp programs aim toward the well-rounded development of the constituents, although a variety of basic emphases may be chosen. Some stress health and physical fitness. A few consider social development as primary. Still others emphasize the development of self-reliance and resourcefulness.

A dominant trend in church encampments is that of

providing spiritual development through religious education, inspiration, and fellowship. Many of them are described as Christian education centers away from home,
close to nature, and for all ages. The stated purpose in the
report of a study committee for a large denomination in
Kentucky is "to provide a statewide fellowship of all Kentucky Baptists for missionary, educational, evangelistic,
and recreational purposes of all age groups."

SITE SELECTION

Site selection should be based on a careful study of
needs and of a philosophy that clearly defines the purposes
and objectives, and the site committee should be thoroughly familiar with these purposes and objectives. In
making a careful search for the best location, the committee should seek assistance of anyone who may be able
to help. Those who may be consulted include county
farm agents, road commissioners, chambers of commerce,
state planning commission, and the U. S. Geological Survey.

Advertisements in newspapers may bring valuable
leads. Assistance of a good real estate firm may be helpful
in finding a site. Such help might be especially valuable
in case several pieces of real estate have to be assembled
to make the site adequate.

The committee should try to learn everything possible
about the location being considered. Aerial photographs
reveal much about general characteristics. Topographical
maps may be available from the U. S. Geological Survey.
The committee should seek also to learn whether there is
flooding during rainy seasons, whether the water supply
is reliable throughout the year, and, whether there are unusual hazards to health and safety.

CRITERIA FOR THE SITE

The search for a site should be based on established criteria. Of major importance is the matter of size. Insufficient ground can greatly limit the program and stifle possibilities for growth. A location may have many favorable aspects, but inadequate size may make it unsuitable for a large investment in buildings. Considerable space is needed for buffer areas between buildings. Since most of the constituents will be urbanites, a wilderness atmosphere is quite desirable. The trend is to provide separate areas for boys' and girls' camps as well as the general area for all ages. This requires much space. Some authorities recommend at least one acre per camper. Effective encampments have been developed on less ground, but every effort should be made to get adequate land. Insurance should be provided against encroachment by undesirable developments.

The shape of the land is also important. A long narrow strip makes the development of an over-all plan more difficult. A divided site hinders planning and also presents problems of protection and management. A site should, if at all possible, be in one piece and have considerable length and breadth.

The best results will be achieved if the location is sufficiently accessible to reduce travel time and cost. Grounds that are intended to serve local groups should be reachable within one or two hours. Denominational assemblies designed to serve larger areas should be reachable within one or two days. Access roads that are publicly maintained are quite desirable. Local fire and police protection, and the availability of doctors and hospitals, always increase the value and attractiveness of a location.

The natural features are of prime importance. Drainage must be adequate. A terrain that slopes in two or more directions is desirable. Marshy places may be a health hazard because of mosquitoes. A variable topography with woods, hills, and ravines, as well as level places, adds to the beauty and the utility. Sandy soil that readily absorbs water greatly reduces the mud factor. Sticky clay requires hard surface walks. Clay can also make much more difficult the proper disposal of waste water and sewage. Few things are more attractive than beautiful streams or bodies of water. The most appealing camp site has an indescribable quality that might be called glamour, and often this is more than natural beauty. It may be related to elevation, climate, or location. Some aspect of the location that suggests an attractive name or slogan usually has strong appeal and thus good public relations value.

ACQUIRING A SITE

The search of the site committee may yield more than one location that meets minimum standards. To be helpful to the sponsoring organization in making a decision, the site committee might prepare written descriptions of advantages and disadvantages of probable first, second, and third choices. If the property must be purchased, the buyer is in a better position to bargain if more than one choice is available. Before authorization to buy is requested, a good job of bargaining should be done. There is a distinct advantage in having the help of a good real estate agent. He will probably know the best approaches and be better able to judge values as well as guard against pitfalls or mistakes. Before the contract is signed, a title search should be made, being sure also to determine whether any easements that would limit the use of the land have been granted.

DEVELOPING THE SITE

Site development should be based on a contour map prepared by a civil engineer. Such a map shows the ground elevation of every part of the site and provides guidance as to where buildings, roads, playgrounds, and all other facilities should be located. Employment of a professional land planner and landscape artist usually is a good investment. The architecture department of denominational agencies often can give expert guidance in this matter.

MASTER PLAN

Before any construction begins, a master plot plan should be designed, carefully considered, and adopted by the sponsoring organization. This design should take into consideration the prospects of achieving long-range objectives as well as goals that are presently obtainable. It should show the most probable location of all anticipated facilities. An advantage of such a master plan is that it gives some assurance that maximum usefulness will ultimately be achieved. It also provides for a unit plan of construction and indicates building priorities that facilitate development by stages. Getting all buildings in proper places and relationships is of great importance.

WATER AND SEWAGE

Of prime importance is the water supply. Before investment in buildings is made, an adequate water supply must be assured. In some locations a stream, lake, or spring may prove to be satisfactory. Of course, a purifying plant is needed to guarantee safe drinking water. Having two systems, one for drinking and another for other purposes, is not a good idea.

Next in importance to the water supply is a suitable system to dispose of sewage. Because of the possible hazard, the state health department has standards that must be met. Pit privies for sewage are cheapest to build and easiest to maintain, but they must be built according to specifications. If these are used, care must be taken to protect the water supply from pollution. Septic tanks can be made adequate but must be built according to health requirements. Larger encampments may prefer to install sewage disposal plants, which usually are more satisfactory but also more expensive.

UTILITIES

Electric power is obtainable almost everywhere now. Natural gas is not so readily available, but many locations are within reach of a pipeline. It is better to grant an easement to the companies for the lines than to construct them privately. Safety standards must be met and maintenance is no small problem. Telephone service is necessary for business and emergencies.

Only necessary roads and drives should be planned. While heavy paving is not required for the lighter traffic, roads should be well engineered to provide proper drainage without washing. Constant repair can be quite expensive. Trails that lead to the beauty spots, to the places of prayer, and to an outdoor amphitheater can be very interesting and popular.

FIRE PREVENTION

In the planning stage every effort should be made to take care of a fire emergency. Plan first for prevention. Proper location of buildings and roads will help to guard against spreading should a fire get started. Water outlets, extinguishers, and other fire-fighting facilities should be provided. One large encampment with a new hotel-type lodge made of cedar and redwood installed a sprinkler system. The manager claims that the savings on insurance premiums will pay for the system in less than ten years. Of course, such a plan requires an adequate supply of water.

Chapter 14

SUMMARY AND REVIEW

THIS BOOK is intended especially for pastors and other staff personnel, both volunteers and employees, who seek further insight and specific guidance in helping their churches obtain and improve real estate. The central purpose is that of providing an educational basis for developing additional competence in this practical application of religious stewardship. No attempt is made to suggest ideas for managing commercial or industrial property.

The material presented herein reflects four basic convictions: First, if churches are to accomplish their distinctive purposes, their approaches to obtaining and improving real estate must be at least as effective as those of other organizations. Second, some of the principles of management that are applied satisfactorily in acquiring and developing real estate for business, government, hospitals, and other situations may be used appropriately and effectively by churches. Third, since churches are service-rendering rather than profit-making, and because of the uniqueness of their voluntary nature and trustee relationship, some of their approaches to real estate management must be different from those of commercial enterprises. Fourth, the differences between management principles as applied to acquisition and development of real estate for secular organizations and management principles as applied to the peculiar needs of churches should be clearly identified and thoroughly understood.

Church buildings and grounds are facilitating resources and should be regarded not as ends in themselves but as important means to an end. Facilities are supposed to strengthen, support, and reinforce the church's avowed objectives and goals. Recalling a basic principle of management, that "form should follow function," we can readily see that facilities relate to *form,* whereas objectives and goals relate to *function.*

Congregations sometimes seem to forget that the establishment of function should precede the designing of form. Thus, instead of acquiring desired facilities, they invite difficulties that could be avoided by determining needs before endeavoring to fill them. For this reason, churches considering a program of real estate expansion should begin with a study committee rather than with a building committee.

People tend to support what they are interested in and to oppose what they do not understand. Information and knowledge often lead to understanding which frequently stimulates support. If the church has something worthy of support, then the story must be told. Pertinent information must be conveyed effectively and constantly.

Various means are available for communicating a church's concept of its objectives, goals, accomplishments, potentialities, and needs. Chief among these means could be a definite program of specific training. Both clergy and laity usually need systematic preparation for the task of obtaining and improving church real estate.

Following are some questions that, if studied diligently and answered comprehensively, should lead to a deeper appreciation of the process of acquiring and developing church real estate within a context of predetermined religious purposes, objectives, and goals. Some of the questions are framed in such a way as to require the reader to consider particular situations.

1. In what significant respects should a church's approach to acquisition and improvement of real estate differ from that of (a) other nonprofit charitable organizations, (b) commercial establishments, (c) government agencies? In what significant respects should the approach be either similar or identical?

2. In what ways should a church's approach to obtaining and developing real estate be determined by (a) its voluntary nature, (b) its trustee relationship? In what respects should these two characteristics make no particular difference?

3. Of the various reasons given for the importance of careful study and planning for expansion of church real estate facilities, what are the two that seem to be most significant for your own situation? Explain.

4. What are two of the basic functions of the church, as stated by Jesus? What should be the relationship between these functions and the development of church real estate?

5. Why should a church make a self-study of its distinctive purposes and unique opportunities before developing plans for real estate expansion? What favorable results may come from such a study?

6. What are some of the community agencies that may be helpful to a church in making a self-study? What kinds of help may be available from each of these agencies?

7. Suggest a procedure by which any church may analyze its own community in regard to church boundaries, popu-

lation, religious composition, economic prospects, and family and home conditions.

8. What values could accrue to your church through a careful self-study of its membership, its community, and its buildings? What dangers are certain to be faced if guesses or loose estimates are relied upon?

9. The statement is made that it is more important to know the reasons for building than to know what to build. If you agree with this statement, give your reasons. If you disagree, tell why.

10. What precautions should be observed in accepting a gift site? List the chief characteristics of a good location. Compare this list with the strengths and weaknesses of your own church location.

11. Of what value should the work of the study committee be to the work of the site committee? Since a major expansion project should be the work of the whole congregation, how may the responsibility be distributed?

12. The size of the building committee and the method of selecting it should depend on the size and polity of the congregation. What size and method would be most suitable in your own situation?

13. In a small church, where leadership may be limited, a full list of subcommittees may not be possible. What combination of committee functions would be suitable?

14. A long list of reasons is given for eliminating basements. What six objections seem to you to be most valid?

15. What are the main advantages of a unit plan of construction?

16. Evaluate the proposal that subcommittees on worship, education, administration, and fellowship be responsible for planning for the major functions of the church? Would this division of responsibility be needed in every church?

17. What are some of the most important features of the entrance, narthex, nave, and chancel? What are the advantages and the disadvantages of the divided chancel?

18. It is stated that the basic objectives of Christian education are to impart information, encourage Christian growth, and win believers. How do these compare with the objectives of your church?

19. What important new trends in Christian education should be taken into account as new physical facilities are planned?

20. What advantages accrue to a church when adults are included in the program of Christian education?

21. Churches are planning to meet the recreational needs of their people more than ever before. What are some basic reasons for this new approach?

22. Why should the social room or parish hall not be located under the worship center? Where should it be located for best results?

23. Why has it become unnecessary for churches to provide facilities for preparing extra large meals? How can a large church where more than one social function may be in progress at the same time provide more than one kitchen at a minimum expense?

24. Explain the importance of well-planned administrative facilities. What rooms are needed in an adequate church office, and what would be a suitable arrangement of rooms?

25. In planning floor space, maintenance workers are often forgotten. What should be included in the plans to make their work more effective?

26. For many churches the library has become an important part of the education program. Where should the library be located and what features should be included to ensure its regular use?

27. What are the main reasons for engaging an architect for a program of real estate expansion? Which of the criteria suggested for selection of an architect do you feel are the most important?

28. Why is it important for the church to designate one person as spokesman to deal directly with the architect? Who should this person be?

29. The two basic responsibilities of the finance committee are to raise money and to arrange to borrow money. How soon can it begin to work? What are the elements of a good fund-raising campaign?

30. Of the several suggested methods for raising money, which seem most appropriate for your situation? What are the dangers in a "do-it-yourself" campaign to raise funds?

31. Give reasons for, and reasons against, employing professional help in fund raising. What is your own opinion regarding this matter?

32. In seeking church loans, it is extremely important to make good preparation. What steps are required? Where can a finance committee look for a loan? How much can a church afford to borrow?

33. The selling of church bonds, or "income financing," is a method used by many churches. What are the advantages and the difficulties of this method?

34. Two methods are used to assure a clear title to real estate. What are they? Which of the two offers better protection?

35. What are some of the problems that may be encountered because of restrictions and other title encumbrances?

36. What are some of the reasons for carrying liability insurance and a guaranty bond? What other types of insurance are needed to adequately protect a congregation while a building is under construction?

37. What is the basic purpose of the construction committee and through whom should it work to achieve its purpose?

38. Why is it important to have a selected list of prospective bidders?

39. The contractor is entitled to payments on the building as it is in process of completion. How should these payments be equitably and legally provided for?

40. What are the responsibilities of the construction committee after completion of the building?

41. What conditions have caused the church-owned parsonage tradition to persist? What new conditions are encouraging a shift to a pastor-owned home? Arguments are given on both sides of this question. Which do you feel have more merit?

42. What special considerations should be taken into account when seeking the location for a parsonage?

43. What unique features should be planned for the pastor's home to make it livable for his family as well as efficient for his ministry?

44. What are some of the important questions that should be answered before starting an encampment program?

45. What are some unworthy ways of getting an encampment program started? Describe the ideal way.

46. What are some of the dominant trends in the rapidly growing movement toward camp development?

47. Several criteria for a suitable encampment location are suggested. Which of these do you consider to be especially important?

48. What officers or agencies might be in a position to advise an encampment site committee? In acquiring a site, what caution should be taken in regard to titles?

49. What significant developments or trends in acquisition and development of church real estate do you predict or suggest for the decade immediately ahead? Why?

SOURCES OF FURTHER

INFORMATION

Books:

ANDERSON, MARTIN, *A Guide to Church Building and Fund Raising*. Minneapolis: Augsburg Press, 1959.

ATKINSON, C. HARRY, *How to Get Your Church Built*. Garden City, N.Y.: Doubleday & Company, Inc., 1964.

GRAVES, ALLEN W., *Using and Maintaining Church Property*. Englewood Cliffs, N.J.: Prentice-Hall, Inc., 1965.

HARRELL, W. A., *Planning Better Church Buildings*. Nashville: Convention Press, 1957.

SCOTFORD, JOHN R., *When You Build Your Church*. Manhasset, N.Y.: Channel Press, Inc., 1958.

SHEAR, JOHN KNOX, ed. *Religious Buildings for Today*. New York: F. W. Dodge Corporation, 1957.

Site Selection and Development: Camps—Conferences—Retreats. The National Council of Churches of Christ in the U.S.A., Philadelphia: United Church Press, 1965.

Magazines:

Church Management. 13308 Euclid Avenue, Cleveland, Ohio.

Protestant Church Buildings and Equipment. 27 East 39th Street, New York, N.Y.

Your Church: Its Buildings—Equipment—Administration—

and Finances. The Religious Publishing Co., 122 Old York Road, Jenkintown, Pa.

Church Headquarters Offices:

The American Baptist Convention, Department of Church Architecture, Valley Forge, Pa.

The Methodist Church, Department of Church Architecture, 1701 Arch Street, Philadelphia 3, Pa.

The National Council of Churches of Christ in the U.S.A., 475 Riverside Drive, New York, N.Y. (In addition to the proceedings of each annual conference on church architecture and church building, many helpful pamphlets are available.)

Southern Baptist Sunday School Board, Church Architecture Department, Nashville, Tenn. 37203.

The United Lutheran Church in America, Department of Church Architecture, 231 Madison Avenue, New York, N.Y.

The United Presbyterian Church in the U.S.A., Board of National Missions, Division of Church Building Aid, 475 Riverside Drive, New York, N.Y.

Index

INDEX